Authors in Their

This book is due for return on or before the last date shown below.

THOMAS HARDY

Authors in Their Age

THOMAS HARDY

Christopher Walbank

BLACKIE

BLACKIE & SON LIMITED
Bishopbriggs Glasgow G64 2NZ
Furnival House 14–18 High Holborn London WC1V 6BX

For Frank and Mary Walbank, my parents

Cover photograph of Thomas Hardy by R. Grenville Eves
reproduced by courtesy of The Toucan Press, Guernsey

Printed in Great Britain by
Thomson Litho Ltd, East Kilbride, Scotland

Authors in Their Age

Authors in Their Age is a series of introductions to the work of major authors in English literature. Each book provides the background information that can help a reader see such an author in context, involved in and reacting to the society of which he was a part.

Some volumes are devoted to individual authors such as Chaucer and Wordsworth. Others look at a particular period in our literary history in which an author can be seen as representative of his time—for example, *The Age of Keats and Shelley* and *The Age of Lawrence*.

There is no attempt to impose a standard format on each of the books. However, all the books provide biographical material and deal with the important political, social and cultural movements of the time. Each book considers the author's readership, the problems of editing his or her work and the major influences on his or her writing. All are well illustrated with drawings, documents or photographs of the time.

There is also a guide to further reading and other source material which will enable the student to progress to a more detailed study of the writer's work and its treatment by literary critics.

Anthony Adams
Esmor Jones
General Editors

The author wishes to thank the following for their help and assistance during the preparations of *Thomas Hardy*: the Master and Fellows of Clare College, Cambridge; the Headmaster and staff of Dartington Hall school, Devon; the Dartington Hall Trustees; his parents, Frank and Mary Walbank; Dorothy Crawford and Andrew Hutchison; Mr R. N. R. Peers, Curator of Dorset County Museum, and his staff.

Contents

I

A Biographical Sketch

INTRODUCTORY

Thomas Hardy died in his eighty-eighth year, a national figure, honoured by literary and academic worlds alike, the friend of royalty and the aristocracy. There are enormous contradictions in this man's character: between the man who places such value on the lifestyle of the old rural village community and yet hotfoots out of it into a milieu of social respectability; between the man who continues to read his Bible throughout his life, regularly attends Anglican services and is the intimate friend of innumerable parsons and bishops and yet who condemns outmoded and superstitious religious beliefs; between the passionate lives and expressions of his literary creations and the quiet, meticulous, respectable man of habit who, throughout his life, disliked being touched.

Most of what we know of his well-documented life comes from a biography written by his second wife Florence from notes prepared for it by Hardy himself. We should not be too harsh on Hardy for wanting to interpret his own life to posterity. It is too easy to note the deception involved, the omission from the biography of love affairs and reference to the obscurity of his social origins, and see him as some sort of social-climbing hypocrite. We must remember that he was writing at a time when probing a man's intimate life was considered neither proper nor desirable: his reticence in some areas may have been motivated by dictates of good taste. His desire to show himself as a member of an old, landed, Dorset family that had fallen on hard times must be understood in the context of those times: although Hardy wrote in the 1920s he is really a Victorian in his desire for respectability.

CHILDHOOD AND YOUTH

Thomas Hardy was born on 2 June 1840, in a cottage at the top of a lane which constituted the hamlet of Higher Bockhampton in the parish of Stinsford. Stinsford (the Mellstock of the novels), with its church and the great house of Kingston Maureward where Hardy's father worked as a master mason, was a few fields away, and from there it was no more than a couple of miles along the river path into Dorchester. Behind the cottage was a plantation, and beyond that the open heath.

The labour was a difficult one and the child was left for dead until it was noticed by the nurse in attendance that he was still breathing. It was thought that he was unlikely to live long.

Jemima Hardy (*née* Hand), his mother, had been married five months when he was born. She emerges from the biographies as a figure of considerable strength and imagination. Orphaned at an early age and brought up on parish relief, she had met her husband while working as cook to the Vicar of Maiden Newton. Her own mother had been the daughter of a yeoman farmer and it was from her that she gained the great love of reading which she passed on to her son. Several entries in the biography suggest that she spent a lot of time with him, playing, encouraging his childish games, introducing him early to the fantasy worlds of song, verse and story and encouraging him to become as involved as possible in the enthusiasms and pursuits of his father.

Thomas Hardy, senior, was a man content with his lot in life as a master mason. Their cottage, built by his father (also a mason), was freehold, and he had a regular assured income from a job he enjoyed in a place he loved. At one time he had ten men in his employment. He could have made more money if he had moved into Dorchester, but this would have taken him away from his friends and interests outside his job. He was a skilled fiddler. Young Thomas could tune a fiddle from a tender age and would accompany his father when he went to play at gatherings of friends. It was a musical family. Hardy's grandfather had founded the parish choir of instrumentalists which, although it had no wind like Puddletown choir, was accounted to be the finest in the district. This choir was disbanded when Hardy was two, but his father would often play the settings of hymns and metrical psalms copied for the choir, and doubtless these simple tunes (by Tate and Brady) were among the first that the boy learnt to play himself. He recalls the intense delight with which

Thomas Hardy, aged 30, 1870 (by courtesy of Dorset County Museum and the Trustees of the Thomas Hardy Memorial Collection)

he would listen to his father playing the folk tunes of country dances. The house was stocked with the sheet music of his father and his grandfather. The enthusiasm of both father and son is seen in young Thomas's fourth birthday present from his father, an accordion.

Stinsford church was a focal point in the life of the family. At services there Thomas heard the words of the Bible and Book of

Common Prayer which he was to continue to read for pleasure throughout his life, and in the hymns of Isaac Watts he heard the metrical forms which he was later to use in many of his own verses. He dreamed of becoming a parson and, when bad weather prevented church attendance, he would don a tablecloth and enact a mock service for his mother.

His sister Mary, to whom he was especially close, was born when he was one. He had one brother, Henry (born 1851), and the youngest of the family, Katharine, was born when he was sixteen. Thomas was the only one to marry.

At the age of eight he was sent to a new village school, a Church of England foundation, run by Julia Augusta Martin, wife of the owner of the Kingston Estate. She had a particular affection for this frail, sensitive child who was already showing unusual ability. Here he learnt arithmetic and geography. At home his mother had given him Dryden's translation of Virgil's *Aeneid*, Dr Johnson's *Rasselas* and a translation of St Pierre's *Paul and Virginia*, and it is clear that she was not content to leave his education to the school. Hardy acknowledges the deep affection that he developed for Mrs Martin, '*almost that of a lover*', but he was to remain her pupil for only one year. The school to which the ambitious Mrs Hardy now sent her son was in Dorchester and run by a nonconformist group. It is said that the personal affront that Mrs Martin felt had been offered to her was the cause of Hardy's father losing work on the Estate. The number of times that Hardy returns in his biography to his early feelings for Mrs Martin shows that this was a relationship of some intensity for him. It is likely that he first felt then the gap between the social classes which was to become a major theme of the novels.

At Isaac Last's Academy in Dorchester, to which he walked three miles each day, he made unusual progress. Hardy excelled in Latin, which was offered as an extra, and won prizes. It was lucky for him that this was one of the few country schools that offered any education beyond the age of thirteen or fourteen. He stayed at Last's Academy until he was sixteen.

Without understanding Dorchester of this period it is impossible to comprehend the formative nature of his schooldays there. It was a country town, busy with the traffic of carts, animals, market-men and merchants. It was a county town with its assize courts, its jail and its public hangings (Hardy himself witnessed two public hangings in his youth, one of which was of

Dorchester Fair, 1835, from the painting by Frederick Barry, engraved by Newton Fielding (by courtesy of Dorset County Museum and the Trustees of the Thomas Hardy Memorial Collection)

a girl who had murdered her husband in circumstances not unlike those in *Tess of the d'Urbervilles*). It was a garrison town of the Dorsetshire Cavalry (known as 'The Blues') with the parades, the bands, the uniforms and all the romance that this suggests. It was a changing town. The railway came to Dorchester in 1847, bringing with it not only news and people and the music-hall ballads that were to supersede genuine folk song, but also new agricultural machinery and chemical fertilizers. With the advent of the railway there was speedy dispersal of dairy products: this favoured the expansion of the dairy farms.

The Tolpuddle Martyrs, who had been transported in 1834 for holding a trade union meeting in defiance of the law, came from a village some five miles north of Hardy's home. When transportation was abolished in 1850, a new solution to the problem of housing long-term criminals was found in the erection of large, fortress-like jails. Hardy saw the Portland jail being constructed with forced criminal labour. In order to reach Portland to lay the foundation stone in July 1849, Prince Albert had to leave the railway at Dorchester and proceed by coach. This fleeting visit is recorded in *The Mayor of Casterbridge*.

Hardy was thirteen when the third great cholera epidemic came to Dorchester. The infection had been caused by the evacuation of infected prisoners from the Millbank jail in London to the Dorchester Cavalry barracks. In the midst of the death and suffering, the railway that had brought them must have been seen as a very mixed blessing.

Always evident in the streets in and around Dorchester was the great poverty of the labouring classes. They were virtually a slave class, underpaid, living in tied cottages from which they could be evicted at a moment's notice, dependent for sustenance either on the kindness of their employers or on poaching. The violent community at the bottom edge of the town that bred such conditions was later portrayed by Hardy in his description of Mixen Lane in *The Mayor of Casterbridge*. The social injustice that such people suffered was one of his life-long concerns. If he learnt it from nowhere else, Hardy could have found enough human suffering and violence in Dorchester of the 1850s and 1860s to account for what his critics have called his pessimistic view of Fate. He would have called it realism.

At home Hardy spent hour after hour reading widely, partly to improve his general education and partly because it had become a passion with him. He read the plays of Shakespeare, was frightened by Apollyon in Bunyan's *Pilgrim's Progress* and found adventure in the novels of Dumas the elder and Harrison Ainsworth. He was still encouraged to accompany his father on his musical engagements at dances, weddings and folk festivals. He would play the fiddle himself and was deeply moved by the simple melodies. Contemporary descriptions of village gatherings suggest that they degenerated on occasions into drunken orgies, and one cannot help but wonder what the impressionable Thomas made of these rough revels.

In the biography Hardy gives us a list of village beauties whom he admired at this period of his life. He is less informative about his feelings for the daughter of a local farmer of some property. At the age of fifteen Hardy was allowed to join the two sons of the Vicar of Stinsford helping the girls in the Bible Class with their studies. He fell in love with Louisa Harding, one of his pupils, one year his junior. When it was discovered, her father forbade her to speak to him, and there we might have expected the matter to have ended: the country boy once more thwarted by the difference of class. In fact, however, he worshipped her from afar for many years. When he came home from his first year in London he tried to see her, and her death in 1913 moved him to write several poems[1] and visit her grave. Hardy's attachments were romantic and cerebral, and appear to have depended little on physical relationship.

What Hardy should do when he left school was undecided, so he joined his father for a short time. Accompanying him on a job restoring Woodsford Castle he met the Dorchester architect, John Hicks, who saw the boy's general ability, gave him a surveying job as a trial and later offered him an apprenticeship. The money was found (Hardy's mother quibbled over the abnormally low fee and knocked Hicks down from £50 to £40), and Hardy started work in Hicks's office in South Street in July 1856 at the age of sixteen.

APPRENTICESHIP IN DORCHESTER (1856–62)

By luck Hardy had entered a setting that was as intellectually stimulating as any he could have found. The architect's office was a place of lively argument and discussion, much of it centering either on the classics, philosophy or religion. Hardy had a good knowledge of basic Christian doctrine and indeed, up to the age of twenty-five, he seriously considered going into the Church. Now, although his faith remained unshaken, he met doubts and questions that demanded careful evaluation. His fellow apprentice, Henry Bastow, was a son of the local Baptist minister: he and Hardy had a lengthy debate on the authority for infant baptism in the Anglican Church.

This was a time of religious ferment nationally. The Genesis myth of creation which had been questioned by the geologists in the 1830s was now exploded in Darwin's theory of evolution published in his *Origin of Species* (1859). From 1857, when Hardy met Horace Moule, what had started as arguments on doctrinal differences with Bastow became involvement in some of the deepest and most disturbing religious arguments of the Victorian age.

Horace Moule came from a respected and illustrious family. His father was the Vicar of the Dorchester suburb of Fordington and had won the admiration and love of the whole town during the 1853 cholera epidemic. With inspired efficiency he had organized the parish, fearless of infection himself, enforcing

Thomas Hardy, aged 16, 1856 (copyright, The Toucan Press)

health regulations, burning infected bedding, burying the dead and providing support and comfort to the living. Later he published eight letters he had sent to Prince Albert, President of the Duchy of Cornwall in which Fordington lay, in which he attempted to make him see his responsibility in this matter. Horatio Mosely Moule, known as Horace, was considered the brightest of the sons (two of whom became bishops and one President and Fellow of Corpus Christi College, Cambridge), but he suffered from debilitating depression. Having studied first at Trinity College, Oxford, he left three years later without a degree. He immediately enrolled at Queens' College, Cambridge and went down in 1858 with the Hulsean Prize for Latin for some work *On Christian Oratory* but still no degree. His depressions were suicidal and he sometimes slept with an open razor under his pillow.

Moule met Hardy during one vacation in his second year at Cambridge and adopted him as an intellectual protégé. From him Hardy received instruction and guidance in philosophy, the arts and the classics to a standard one would be lucky to find in the first degree course in any university. He also introduced him to a literary magazine that Hardy was to read for the rest of his life, *Saturday Review*. Though not a radical journal, it was provocative in its comment on religious matters. Moule's dry academic scepticism is echoed in *Saturday Review's* constant attacks on social and intellectual cant.

Next door to Hicks's office was the school of the Dorset poet and eminent linguist, William Barnes. When Hardy and Bastow wanted any adjudication on any point of grammar they would ask Barnes to settle it. Barnes was a remarkable man who, with love and scholarship, worked to preserve the old, pure Dorset language which he claimed was the original Saxon tongue of the English people. Hardy came to share his serious interest in rustic language and also the habit of noting down old songs and country dances before they were swept away by the popular London culture.

During his apprenticeship Hardy first wrote for publication. His first piece appeared in a Dorchester paper. It was a comic plea in the form of a letter from a clock begging to be returned to its customary place over the Dorchester Almshouses. More personal is the poem 'Domicilium'[2], printed at the end of this chapter, which he wrote on the death of his father's mother in 1857. She had lived with them for years and much of Hardy's knowledge of local lore and stories must have come from her lips.

Hicks was also a classical scholar and he must have enjoyed watching Hardy's intellectual expansion under the influence of Horace Moule, but the main purpose of the boy's presence was to learn architecture. In 1860, while Moule was teaching Hardy enough Greek to enable him to read the tragedies, Hicks was taking him out on the job to assist with church restoration. When Hardy asked Moule for advice about his future career, he was told to stick to architecture: at least it would make him a living. And so, at the age of twenty-one, having completed his initial training, Hardy took the bold step of moving to London to continue training and to work in an office that would provide wider experience than he could get in Dorchester. Through an introductory letter he met Arthur Bloomfield who took him into his office, where he remained for the next five years.

LONDON, ARCHITECTURAL SUCCESS, EARLY POETRY AND HIS FIRST NOVEL (1862–69)

If the move to Dorchester had widened Hardy's horizons, the move to London was even more significant. He now found himself in an *avant-garde* social milieu, among new ideas about society and religion which in many ways anticipated the twentieth century. The boy from Dorset, as can be seen from a photograph taken at the time (see page 11), now becomes the bright, aspirant, young architect and man of the times.

Bloomfield's office was just as convivial as that of Hicks. Hardy sang a weak tenor in the office choir and entertained his colleagues with lunchtime lectures on the great figures of English literature. When they moved to the new office in St Martin's Lane, Hardy and his colleagues sometimes amused themselves by writing satirical comments on a piece of card and lowering it out of the window until it appeared at the window of the Reform League which had rooms below. He secured lodgings, bought a second-hand fiddle and played Verdi with a flatmate who was an adequate pianist.

Outside office hours he was immensely busy fitting in as much as he could. He attended the Royal Opera House at Covent Garden two or three times a week. At home he was working on two projects. At the beginning of 1863 he won both the Architectural Association's Tite Prize for the design of a country mansion and the Royal Institute of British Architects' Silver Medal for his essay 'On The Application of Coloured Bricks and Terra Cotta'. Spurred on by his success he continued his private studies and wide reading.

Moule, by correspondence, still remained his guide as to what he should read in literature as in philosophy and religion. Hardy annotated a copy of Palgrave's *Golden Treasury* that Moule gave him and unsuccessfully tried to accept the arguments of Newman's *Apologia*. In the years 1866 and 1867 Hardy was writing a lot of verse. Many poems were experimental in their vocabulary or verse form; most were sombre in tone and reflected a melancholic turn of mind. The ballad forms of Scott and Meredith are a clear influence, but there is a characteristic resistance to smooth versifying. 'Neutral Tones'[3] was written in the first half of 1867. In a Preface to *Wessex Poems* Hardy points out that although some critics showed resentment when he turned his talents from novels to poetry, many of his poems had

Thomas Hardy, aged 21, 1861 (copyright, The Toucan Press)

been written before he attempted to write a novel. Among his aids to the process of poetic creation were a *Dictionary of Rhyme* and verse skeletons which he wrote out as a means of studying form.

A crisis of religious faith seems to have occurred during 1865 which Dr Gittings[4] associates with a relationship with a girl. Hardy had been reading Comte, whose philosophy sees man, having moved through primitive and metaphysical phases of belief, evolving a new positive (or rational) attitude to God and society. From J. S. Mill he learnt to distrust the irrational, and put faith in reasoned thought. Dr Gittings suggests that Hardy met a girl who, like Sue Bridehead in *Jude the Obscure*, challenged Hardy's doctrinal beliefs. In the book, Sue, following Jowitt in *Essays and Reviews*, rearranges the books of the New

Testament in the order of their historical composition, beginning with the Epistle to the Thessalonians. At the beginning of Hardy's Bible (where he often recorded days on which a particular passage was read or had been heard or what it had suggested to him), there appears the initial H. Writing to his sister Mary that October Hardy asked if he might bring a girlfriend, H. A., to stay with her at Christmas. The evidence is suggestive but slender. Whatever the truth may be, his poems of the time concern disappointment in love and religious doubt. In the same year he was confused as to how to direct his career.

Perhaps as an antidote to depression Hardy pushed himself harder and harder. In October 1865 he enrolled for evening classes in French at King's College. With the idea that a career writing poetry could be combined with a career in the Church he had written to a friend in Cambridge to enquire about entry qualifications, but this came to nothing. How could he honestly study for the ministry with his doubts? In May of the following year he had a brief enthusiasm for the life of the theatre, became star-struck for a time and even got himself a walk-on part in a production of *The Forty Thieves* at Covent Garden.

The pace of life in London, his religious crisis, disappointment in love, confusion about his career; some or all of these things may have been contributory factors to a serious decline in Hardy's health in 1867. Bloomfield's suggestion that he should recuperate in the country coincided with a request from Hicks of Dorchester for a good assistant. The end of July saw Hardy in the cottage at Higher Bockhampton where his energy and vigour soon returned. Much of his disillusionment with London life emerges in his first novel, *The Poor Man and The Lady*, which he started to write while convalescing at Bockhampton. He failed to get the novel published at the time but it was shortened and published some twenty years later under the title *An Indiscretion in the Life of an Heiress*. The original plot concerns a Dorset labourer, Will Strang, who falls in love with a Squire's daughter. He is rejected because of his class, trains as an architect and eventually returns, famous after winning a major architectural prize. He hears that his beloved is to marry a man of the Squire's choosing and the night before the wedding he contrives to meet her in the church. The heroine falls ill and dies after confessing her love for Strang. One cannot ignore the autobiographical parallels. The story is melodramatic and contains situations bitterly critical of middle-class convention. Hardy was advised not to publish it both by Alexander Macmillan (who wrote him a very fair and constructive letter) and George Meredith, reader for Chapman and Hall. Meredith suggested that he should write something more in the Wilkie Collins line with a more complicated plot, advice he heeded in his next novel *Desperate Remedies*.

TRYPHENA SPARKS

Thoughts of Phena
At News of Her Death

Not a line of her writing have I,
    Not a thread of her hair,
No mark of her late time as dame in her dwelling, whereby
    I may picture her there;
    And in vain do I urge my unsight
        To conceive my lost prize
At her close, whom I knew when her dreams were
        upbrimming with light,
    And with laughter her eyes.

What scenes spread around her last days,
    Sad, shining, or dim?
Did her gifts and compassions enray and enarch her sweet
        ways
    With an aureate nimb?
    Or did life-light decline from her years,
        And mischances control
Her full day-star; unease, or regret, or forebodings, or fears
    Disennoble her soul?

Thus I do but the phantom retain
    Of the maiden of yore
As my relic; yet haply the best of her—fined in my brain
    It may be the more
    That no line of her writing have I,
        Nor a thread of her hair,
No mark of her late time as dame in her dwelling, whereby
    I may picture her there.

March 1890

We do not know whether Hardy fell in love with Tryphena Sparks on his return from London or two years later when he worked for Mr Crickmay in Dorchester and then in Weymouth. Tryphena was the youngest daughter of Maria Sparks, the sister of Hardy's mother. On the first occasion she was sixteen and working as a pupil-teacher at the Church of England school at Puddletown. By 1869 she had moved to a school at Coryates, a hamlet to the east of Dorchester. At Coryates she lodged with a farm bailiff and his wife. The owner of the farm was Mrs Catherine Hawkins. Dr Gittings has pointed out the close similarity of this farm run by an enterprising widow to that run by Bathsheba Everdene in *Far from the Madding Crowd*.[5]

In the intervening year, 1868, Hardy had returned to London. His first novel had been rejected and his poetic output virtually died. The opportunity to return to Dorset occurred when, in November 1868, on the death of John Hicks, Hardy was invited by the man who had taken over the firm, Mr G. Crickmay, to help complete the designs left unfinished in the Dorchester office. Greatly impressed by Hardy's designs for the expansion of the early English church at Turnworth, he invited him to work in the main office in Weymouth in 1869.

Hardy enjoyed his life at Weymouth. He bathed in the sea daily, made excursions and rowed in the harbour. Coryates and Tryphena were near. He must have enjoyed rather more independence than he had done living at home. His relationship with Tryphena seems to have blown hot (he bought her a ring) and then curiously cold. Her involvement in family troubles at the time (her sister Martha, who had a job as a lady's maid in Kensington, had become pregnant and lost her job) may have caused strain between them, or perhaps the work that enabled her to be accepted by Stockwell Normal College in London demanded time she might otherwise have spent with Hardy. Entering a residential teachers' training college was rather like taking the veil as regards access to male friends, and this may have been an issue of contention between them. Whatever the cause, he appears to have parted with the dark-haired Tryphena, and after January they deliberately avoided each other. In 1890 Hardy was in a train when suddenly he thought of her. He jotted down a poem[6] in which he described her as his '*lost prize*', unaware of the fact that she was dying at that time. He notes in the 1895 Preface to *Jude the Obscure* that some of the circum-

Tryphena Sparks (copyright, The Toucan Press)

stances were suggested to him by the death of a woman in 1890. However, he firmly denied the suggestion that the novel was autobiographical. The epicene Sue Bridehead in *Jude the Obscure* is clearly not a portrayal of 'Phena, but Fancy Day resembles her in her description and her job as a teacher.[7] The poems 'At Rushy Pond'[8] and 'The Mound' almost certainly refer to her. What is interesting is the degree to which Hardy used the women he had known and loved as ideas and types in his novels. The character of Sue Bridehead is probably drawn from the daughter of Lord Houghton, Mrs Henniker, whom Hardy met in 1893 and with whom he collaborated on the writing of a short story.

An extraordinary theory about Tryphena which has been proposed by Lois Deacon and Terry Coleman[9] has some support. It is based on much supposition, autobiographical interpretation of the poems and novels to fit the theory, a dramatic death-bed confession of Tryphena's daughter, and some false evidence. That some of the poems refer to moments spent with Tryphena is certain. The rest of the theory verges on the fantastic. Briefly it is that Rebecca Sparks (brought up as Tryphena's sister) was in fact the child of Hardy's mother and father, born before they were married. That much is possible. Miss Deacon then suggests that Tryphena was Rebecca's illegitimate daughter brought up as her sister. Hardy fell in love with Tryphena and she became pregnant. Their relationship ended tragically when Hardy's mother revealed that Tryphena was not really his cousin but his niece! Miss Deacon interprets most of Hardy's literary output as an agonized confession of his dark secret to posterity. The theory suggests that the illegitimate son, Randolph, was brought up by Tryphena and the man she married, Charlie Gale. There is no written evidence for the existence of this child. Anyone who wishes to see how a myth can be created out of half-truth, poetic licence and enthusiasm should read Dr Gittings' appendix on the subject.[10]

EMMA GIFFORD, EARLY NOVELS, SUCCESS AND MARRIAGE

In March 1870 Hardy went down to St Juliot's, a parish in north Cornwall, to do some drawings for the restoration of the church. At the rectory where he stayed he met the sister of the Rector's young wife. Emma Gifford was the youngest daughter of a retired Plymouth solicitor who had moved to Bodmin on the death of his wife. In later years she considered herself to be from a better social class than Hardy: her uncle became Archdeacon of London. Hardy appears to have kept particulars about his own family well into the background during their courtship and, indeed, after. She was only a few months younger than Hardy and one can see why it was likely that in the long, hot summer of 1870, during Hardy's regular visits to supervise the restoration work, they should fall deeply in love. She was an attractive woman, blue-eyed, full-bosomed, and with masses of golden hair. Her great vitality and gaiety must have been rather lost on the parishioners of St Juliot's. She sang well, was a skilled rider and was better read than many ladies of the time. To Emma Gifford Hardy must have seemed a romantic character; a successful

Emma Gifford, 1870, as she was when Hardy met her at St Juliot's, Cornwall. '*She opened the door of the West to me.*' (by courtesy of Dorset County Museum and the Trustees of the Thomas Hardy Memorial Collection)

architect who was well acquainted with London and its social life, a serious thinker with advanced views on the great questions of the age and a wry sense of humour. Emma too was a serious woman. Under her influence Hardy resumed regular church attendance. We get a strong picture of her from the rush of poems Hardy wrote after the shock of her death in 1912 which he called 'Veteris Vestigia Flammae'.

His second novel, *Desperate Remedies*, was turned down by Macmillan but accepted by Tinsley Brothers on the condition that Hardy paid £75 to cover loss. Since he possessed only £123 this was a brave venture. In fact he was to get back all but £15 of it. He was back in Weymouth working for Crickmay when, in May 1871, a slating review appeared in the *Spectator*. It required the joint efforts of Emma and Horace Moule (who had just returned to Dorchester after two years teaching at Marlborough) to persuade Hardy not to give up writing altogether. Acute sensitivity to criticism never left him even when he was an established man of letters. The novel is indeed melodramatic but it is well constructed and has some memorable scenes.

Favourable comments had been made in reviews about his portrayal of rustic characters. Accordingly he set his next novel in Stinsford, working much rustic detail round a simple country

Stinsford church (Mellstock in the novels) where Hardy's father and grandfather played in the church band. Hardy's heart is buried here, between the graves of his two wives.

romance and the fate of the Mellstock choir. He wrote it in Bockhampton in the summer of 1871 and Emma helped him to copy it out. It was accepted by Macmillan for publication in the following year. However, he seems to have been in some doubt as to whether it was to be published and, discouraged, he gained new architectural employment in London designing schools for the London Schools Board.

The next year, 1872, brought him some recognition as a novelist. *Under the Greenwood Tree* appeared in April. Tinsley waited for the critical reaction (which was moderately enthusiastic) before offering Hardy £200 for the serial rights of a novel which so far existed only in note form, *A Pair of Blue Eyes*. In September he found that he was not keeping up with the instalments and so gave up his career as an architect and returned to Higher Bockhampton to complete the novel. His heroine is closely modelled on Emma. They had visited her father, the retired solicitor, at his home in Bodmin during August. He had disapproved of Hardy because of his working-class origins. Their love was undiminished but it was true that they could not possibly get married on his present income. Financial success was not to come until the following year with the publication of *Far from the Madding Crowd* in Leslie Stephen's *Cornhill Magazine*.

After reading *Under the Greenwood Tree* Stephen had written to Hardy requesting a story for his magazine, and most of 1873 was spent writing it. Most Victorian novelists had their work first published in serial form in literary journals, and editors had considerable power. A former university don, Leslie Stephen was no simple publisher. Among his own works were the first edition of *The National Dictionary of Biography* and scholarly works on Pope and Swift. He published an article explaining his agnosticism in *Fraser's Magazine*. He had strong critical values and also knew what his readers wanted. Hardy meekly obeyed his instructions to pack more action into this novel and put a dramatic peak in each episode. Hardy found in Stephen an invaluable critic whose judgment on what held up the story or what was good was invariably sound. He was to be a good personal friend to Hardy and an influence on him both as a writer and in the development of his religious thought. In some respects Stephen was to fill the role previously played by Moule.

In June of that year Hardy and his brother Henry visited Horace Moule in Cambridge. They dined in Queens' College and Moule took them up onto the roof of King's College chapel. A poem, 'Standing By The Mantelpiece',[11] recalls their last supper together. The white shroud on the guttering candle is ominous. It was the last time that they met. In September Hardy was shocked to hear of Horace Moule's suicide in his rooms at Queens' College. In a state of deep despair and with his brother in the room next door he had eventually carried out his frequent threat to cut his throat with a razor. Hardy attended the funeral at Fordington. Some release from his grief must have been found in the demands of his writing. Through the autumn and winter he continued to work in his room in the cottage at Bockhampton on *Far from the Madding Crowd*. The moving description of the death of Fanny Robin may owe something to his feelings of loss.

With illustrations by Helen Paterson, the first episode of *Far from the Madding Crowd* was published in December 1873. Hardy was surprised to see that it was accorded the front position in the magazine when he bought a copy in Dorchester on returning from a visit to St Juliot's. The story was widely acclaimed. Its success owes much to the advice of Stephen but also to a new personal confidence. There had been an element of mockery in his portrayal of the rustics in *Under the Greenwood Tree* which Hardy later regretted: the rustics in *Far from the Madding Crowd* are handled more seriously; they are part of the backcloth of realism and continuity against which we see the fated strivings of the lovers. The hiring fair and the poorhouse are not romantic: there is a new concern here for social realism. There is also a new symbolic strength in several scenes: the sword-drill, and the great storm in which Bathsheba almost loses all her ricks. Similarly the hiring scene, the shearing scene and the medication of the clover-blown sheep show us, rather than describe, Oak's relationship to his environment. Hardy did not let Emma see this novel until it was complete, possibly because some of the scenes reflect the poverty of his mother's early circumstances. He was delighted with the story's success but angry that it was attributed by some to the hand of George Eliot. For all her strength he felt that she could not possibly have had such first-hand knowledge of Dorset.

Flushed with success and with a more secure income Hardy could now afford to marry. Emma and he were married by her uncle in St Peter's Church, Paddington on 17 September 1874. Only two of her relatives were present and none of Hardy's— neither his mother nor his father, not even his sister Mary. The only inference that I can make to explain this is the sad possibility that he made them feel that it would be better if they did not come. This, after all, was not a country wedding!

STURMINSTER NEWTON (1876–78)

On their return from a honeymoon in France the Hardys found lodgings in Surbiton, London. The story that Hardy was ostracized by Emma's family is based on a letter Emma's father sent at this point, in which he expressed indignation that Hardy had presumed to marry into the Gifford family. However, their relationship with Canon Gifford who had married them seems to have been cordial. Hardy inscribed a copy of *Far from the Madding Crowd* to him when it came out in book form. All the reviews were favourable except for one written for *The Times* by Henry James. Hardy, characteristically, never forgave him. He scores off him several times in the biography. Delighted when James was not elected to the Rabelais Club, and having taken him there as a guest, Hardy commented: *'he has a ponderously warm manner of saying nothing in infinite sentences'*. Elsewhere, James and Stevenson are described as the *'Osric and Polonius'* of the novelists.

The success of *Far from the Madding Crowd* led Stephen to press Hardy for another story for serial publication. Putting aside an idea for a woodland story, he petulantly determined to write a story that nobody could mistake for the work of George Eliot. The resulting serial story, *The Hand of Ethelberta*, is a society comedy of manners. It started in the *Cornhill Magazine* in May 1875. At this time he noted in his diary that he regarded the production of a new incident for each episode to be hack-writing. He also found the observation of London society for subject matter to be a tedious occupation. Another note concerns a visit to the Chelsea Pensioners where he listened to their reminiscences of the Napoleonic Wars. The idea for a Napoleonic epic (which later became *The Dynasts*) also appears in 1875.

During a holiday in Swanage the Hardys started house-hunting. Hardy was finding London an increasing strain. They found nothing suitable that summer but, with *Ethelberta* completed the following January, they felt that they could devote more time and effort to it and in March 1876 they took lodgings in Yeovil. *Ethelberta* was not given a good critical reception, which Hardy put down to the fact that the public was not yet ready for a comedy of high society at that date: that the plot is incredible and far-fetched seems a much more obvious reason.

By May they had still found nothing suitable in the Yeovil area, and at the end of May they went on holiday to Holland and the Rhine Valley. On the way back they stopped at Brussels where Hardy explored the battlefield of Waterloo and spent a couple of days trying to trace the exact location of the Duchess of Richmond's Ball. On his return he again visited the Chelsea Pensioners to discuss his observations. By the end of June they had found a house they liked, '*a pretty cottage overlooking the Dorset Stour*'[12] at Sturminster Newton. In fact it is a sizeable gabled grey house, a far cry from his parents' cottage in Bockhampton.

The two-year period of his life that followed was both creative and happy. Hardy refers to it as their '*Sturminster idyll*'.[13] His notes at the time contain many anecdotes of folklore, super-stitions he had come across and simple observations of the countryside around him. He had made notes about the Christmas hobby-horse when they visited his parents that Christmas. Much of this detail appears in *The Return of the Native* which he started early in 1877 and which was published in the monthly magazine *Belgravia* during 1878. Though the plot is contrived, this is the most unified of Hardy's novels. The action all takes place on Egdon Heath, and its eighteen months' duration is marked by seasonal activities which are completely integrated into the plot: the autumn bonfire on Rainbarrow, the Christmas mumming, the Midsummer gypsying, the winter floods and the Maypole dancing. The setting of the heath (a fictional area based on the heathland that stretched out behind the Bockhampton cottage) and the lives of its inhabitants were well known to Hardy: the personal tensions of Tamsin, Eustacia, Wildeve and especially Clym, reflect Hardy's feelings towards that life. In returning to the heath after his job in Paris, Clym is responding to the call of the simple, natural life, but nature is also cruel. It takes away Clym's sight and reduces him to uniformity with the heath in his furze-cutter's clothes. It kills Mrs Yeobright, and eventually the swollen waters of the River Frome drown Eustacia and Wildeve at Shadwater Pool. The novel also fills in another part of the map of Wessex first introduced in *Far from the Madding Crowd*.

A diary entry for 13 August 1877, reads:

> *We hear that Jane, our late servant, is soon to have a baby.*
> *Yet never a sign of one is there for us.*[14]

How Hardy would have enjoyed a child and how much a child would have learnt from his love of music, his fund of stories and his knowledge of the countryside. But I doubt that a man with children could have written the baptism scene of little Sorrow in *Tess*,[15] created the character of Little Father Time in *Jude*[16] or contrived Jude's terrible death. Two quotations from poems written during the stay at Sturminster convey something of his happiness:

> *Lifelong to be*
> *Seemed the fair colour of the time*[17]

and of Emma,

> *And beneath the roof is she who in the dark world shows*
> *As a lattice-gleam when midnight moans.*[18]

They returned to London in March 1878 because Hardy felt that a novelist had to live among other writers, and also because they could not afford financially to live away from the literary hub.

FAME, ILLNESS AND A RETURN TO DORSET (1878–81)

The Trumpet Major had been begun before *The Return of the Native* but was completed in London. In order to get the background of the Napoleonic Wars correct, Hardy spent a lot of time in the British Museum. He also made a special visit to Weymouth to verify the setting. It came out in serial form during 1880. It is an underpowered novel with rather conventional characters (Squire Derriman and Festus, for example) and a dragging plot. Much of the story is set at Overcombe Mill where the heroine is brought up, but it fails to carry the symbolic power of Egdon Heath, Mellstock, Talbothays or even Bathsheba Everdene's farm.

By this time Hardy was often to be found at the gatherings of London's cultured. At society dinner parties he met the famous of the age. He joined the Savile Club and was elected to the Rabelais Club as '*the most virile writer of works of the imagination now in London*'. He began writing *A Laodicean* but he and Emma spent much of the year travelling in Normandy, visiting Dorset and then Cambridge on their return. On the day that *The Trumpet Major* was published as a book they returned to London and Hardy took to his bed unwell. Internal bleeding was to lay him up for the next six months. Fearing for his death he strived to finish the novel in hand in order to provide for Emma. The deaths of George Eliot on 22 December and Thomas Carlyle on 4 February depressed him:

> *Both he and George Eliot have vanished into nescience while I have been lying here,* he wrote.[19]

In that use of the word '*nescience*' and in comments in his diary at the time, we can see a struggle taking place with contemporary religious ideas. Near Harfleur on the French trip they had come across a crucifix which was tottering in the wind on a gusty day. He wrote:

> ... *and as it rocked in the wind like a ship's mast Hardy thought that the crudely painted figure of Christ upon it seemed to writhe and cry in the twilight: 'Yes, Yes! I agree that this travesty of me and my doctrines should totter and overturn in this modern world.*[20]

He saw the Church as a travesty but he also thought that the modern world merited the shattering of its beliefs. Retaining his belief in Christ's centrality he mused during his illness on Comte's exclusion of Christ from his list of worthies.

When they moved back to Dorset, to a house in Wimborne Minster, at the end of the year, Hardy recognized that this was not entirely for health reasons. He was depressed by London and knew that he found most inspiration in the countryside of Dorset. A grand tour of Scotland was intended to be recuperative. In September he corrected the proofs of *A Laodicean* and by the end of 1881 he had started work on *Two on a Tower*.

MAX GATE AND THE REMAINING NOVELS (1882–95)

After his illness Hardy had decided to make Dorset his permanent home. Now a pattern of life emerges that the Hardys were to follow for many years: work on a novel in Dorset, the London season (which Mrs Hardy looked forward to more than her husband) and then various holidays travelling.

Two on a Tower appeared during 1882. It is another light social comedy but with some strong rural episodes. Its success, and money coming in from book sales of the previous novels, enabled Hardy to buy a plot of land on the Weymouth Road on the edge of Dorchester, and there he set about building a large and imposing brick house to his own design, Max Gate. Emma would have preferred to live in London.

A study of Hardy's work as a novelist by Havelock Ellis was published in 1883 and this contributed greatly to Hardy's reputation. Ellis notes the uniquely detailed portrait that Hardy gives us of agricultural life and the labouring class. In an article in *Longman's Magazine* of the same year called 'The Dorsetshire Labourer', Hardy sets out to explain the realities of life for the labourer, dismissing the popular misguided notion of Hodge, the funny yokel. He describes the labourers' cottages, their fate at hiring fairs, and pays detailed attention to the Lady Day removals of those who have lost or changed their jobs. He also expresses concern that migration of labour is causing the loss of the old traditions. The same point is made in the biography for the year 1888 where he notes:

> *Labourers formerly, knowing they were permanent residents would plant apple-trees and fruit-bushes with zealous care, to profit from them: but now they scarce ever plant one, knowing they will be finding a home elsewhere in a year or two.*[21]

While Max Gate was being built they lived in Dorchester and Hardy began work on *The Mayor of Casterbridge*. Not under contract to any publisher he was able to finish this in his own time. The novel gives us a vivid picture of Dorchester in the 1850s. The character of Henchard has a complexity that is a new departure. The novel was completed in April 1885 and they moved into Max Gate in June. Success of *The Mayor of Casterbridge* was immediate, and after appearing in serial form in the *Graphic* it was published as a book both in England and America. The next three novels are set locally and although his final novel, *Jude the Obscure*, takes us into a world of railways, training college, university and modern thinking, the hero is a man attempting to escape his country origins.

The biography provides us with a visual portrait of Hardy at the age of 45: 5 foot 6½ inches in height, with a moustache, broad temples and a habit of walking rapidly. He was spare but not thin and never allowed himself to be weighed because he considered it unlucky. We may imagine him with earth on his hands planting the trees in the garden at Max Gate, trees that now shade the house completely, some two miles away from the cottage across the Frome valley where he was born and where his parents still lived. From the front gate he looked the other way, over to the memorial to Admiral Hardy of Trafalgar.

The Woodlanders was written in 1886; this became Hardy's favourite novel. He tells us in the biography that at that time he considered writing novels 'mere journey-work' and he believed that he had sacrificed too much in his work to the demand for an incident in every episode. More important to him, he claimed, was the research he was doing in the British Museum on *The Dynasts*, and his poetry. It is hard for us to understand this when we recognize the personal nature of much of the writing in the novels. *The Woodlanders* contains several themes that are derived from Hardy's own personal experience. The heroine, Grace Melbury, has been uprooted from her country origins by a boarding-school education. She marries a new doctor and thus aligns herself with the world outside that is encroaching on and changing the woodland village of Little Hintock. At the opposite pole of the book is the description of various country people who live and work in this wooded part of the North Dorset Downs to the north of Dorchester. Giles Winterborne, planting trees, or standing under the apple tree he has mounted on his cart to declare his trade in the market, or making cider in the yard outside a Sherton Abbas Hotel in the golden, evening light, embodies the country values and affinity with living things which Grace has lost. Society is seen as cruel and harsh over the specific issues of the power of landowners over the lives of their tenants and the suffering caused by contemporary divorce laws. Fitzpiers echoes Hardy's own belief that marriage is a civil contract that should be ended if it causes suffering to both parties. Nature in the book is powerfully described and is much more fecund and supportive than in *The Return of the Native*. Hardy was hurt that some people found the book indecent and immoral. This was a foretaste of the indignation that was to greet his last two novels.

The Woodlanders was finished in 1887 and soon afterwards Emma and Hardy made a tour of Italy. Friends of the couple sensed a tension between them. Their relationship was to become very badly strained. Emma seems to have come to dislike her husband and then despise him, finding his religious views blasphemous, resenting having to live in Dorchester and regretting that she had married a man of such vulgar social origins. Hardy seems to have withdrawn into himself and his work. A housekeeper at Max Gate recalls that, in the last few years of their marriage, Mr Hardy would come down the back stairs to avoid meeting his wife.[22]

In 1888, after a visit to Paris, Hardy made a start on *Tess of the d'Urbervilles*. Many of his short stories and all those in *A Group of Noble Dames* were written between the publication of *The Woodlanders* and *Tess*.

The first episodes of *Tess* were returned to the writer by the editor of *Murray's Magazine* because of the story's '*improper explicitness*'. Macmillan also declined it. Angry at the misunderstanding of his work Hardy nevertheless set about mutilating the novel, removing parts that were likely to offend and which he could later re-insert for the full volume of the book. His defence of *Candour in English Fiction* was published in 1889 whilst he was preparing *Tess* for serial publication.

An unexplained note appears in his journal for 10 December 1888 which reads:

> *He, she, had blundered ; but not as the Prime Cause had blundered. He, she, had sinned ; but not as the Prime Cause had sinned . . .*[23]

This may refer to Tess and Angel in the new novel or it may be a more personal note. It is one of several items in the biography to illustrate the increasing pessimism of his religious thought. On 29 January 1890 he wrote in his journal:

> *I have been looking for a God for 50 years, and I think that if he had existed I should have discovered him.*[24]

There is the same frank disbelief in a loving God in *Tess*. The novel's famous last paragraph shows Tess as sport for the President of the Immortals:

> *As flies to wanton boys, are we to th' Gods ;*
> *They kill us for their sport.*[25]

Gloucester's words from *King Lear* are recalled several times in the book and Marion and Tess are reduced to the insignificance of flies as they grub for turnips in the rough soil of Flintcomb-Ash. Hardy's religious views also appear in his portrayal of Angel Clare's clerical family and Mercy Chant: they have more propriety than charity. The rapist d'Urberville is swayed to evangelicalism for a time:

> ... the glow on the cheek that yesterday could be translated as riotousness was evangelized to-day into the splendour of pious rhetoric ...[26]

He is as easily persuaded out of his religion as he was persuaded into it. Angel Clare's rejection of Tess at the story's centre is shown to be the result of his repressed Pauline upbringing. But what really angered the prudish when the book appeared was Hardy's tragic heroine, Tess. That the mother of an illegitimate child could be the embodiment of innocence and Apostolic charity horrified many people. Edmund Gosse, on the other hand, wrote to tell Hardy that he heard the book's praises wherever he went. After reading the review in the *Quarterly Review* Hardy noted:

> How strange that one may write a book without knowing what one puts into it—or rather, the reader reads into it. ... Well, if this sort of thing continues, no more novel-writing for me.[27]

The book's notoriety ensured heavy sales. More important in restoring his confidence in novel writing must have been Lionel Johnson's appraisal of his work[28] which appeared at that time.

The Well-Beloved appeared from 1891–92 as a serial. It is a melodramatic story of thwarted love. The artist hero seeks perfection both in woman and in his sculpture. His views on marriage, that an Act of Parliament should not stand in the way of love, anticipate the view that Phillotson arrives at in *Jude the Obscure*. Hardy revised this novel substantially for book publication in 1896.

His father had died in July 1892 and Tennyson in October of the same year. In February 1893 Hardy made arrangements for his father's tombstone with a local mason: this may have suggested the trade of the hero of his last novel, though it was also his father's trade and one in which he himself had some training. There is much of the acute observation of buildings in *Jude the Obscure* that we might expect from a novelist who had trained as an architect and worked with masons on church restoration work. In 1892 he visited Fawley in Berkshire (Marygreen in the novel) and in June 1893 attended a degree ceremony in Oxford (Christminster of the novel). Work on the book progressed through the winter of 1893 during which time Emma was ill. Realizing the hostility that the book was likely to meet, Hardy tried to cancel his contract with *Harper's Bazaar* to produce a serial story. They would not agree and he was again forced to write two versions of the novel, one for serial publication and one for the issue of the complete book. *Jude the Obscure* was a book he felt passionately about, '*something the world ought to be shown*', he wrote in his notebook. The intellectual and social development of Jude follows his own in many respects. The search of Sue and Jude to find love and truth to their emotions is thwarted by society and by a Fate which is indifferent to their sufferings. The harsh criticism in the book of marriage as an indissoluble institution was assumed to be Hardy's own, though he hotly denied this. The Bishop of Wakefield threw his copy onto the fire and wrote to W. F. D. Smith to have the book withdrawn from the circulating libraries. Deeply hurt at its reception, Hardy was at pains to explain that the views of characters in a book are not necessarily those of the author:

> *Of course the book is all contrasts — or was meant to be in its original conception . . . e.g. Sue and her heathen Gods set against Jude's reading of the Greek testament ; Christminster academical, Christminster in the slums ; Jude the saint, Jude the sinner ; Sue the Pagan, Sue the saint ; marriage, no marriage etc.*[29]

Despite *Jude's* popularity — it was very quickly translated into editions in German, French, Russian, Dutch and Italian — Hardy determined to write no more novels. Emma, increasingly devout, was horrified by the book's attack on religion. Their relationship at this time appears to have worsened considerably.

POEMS, THE DYNASTS, HONOURS AND THE DEATH OF EMMA

After revising *The Well-Beloved* in 1886 he took Emma to Switzerland on a holiday. The next year was to be spent preparing his early poems for publication and writing Prefaces for a uniform edition of his novels. *Wessex Poems* was to be published in 1898. In 1897 he had taken to the new sport of cycling and toured the countryside. In September he rode to Weymouth with Rudyard Kipling. This appears to have been a pastime which Emma also enjoyed. In London Hardy continued to work gathering detail for *The Dynasts*. Several of the poems in his next volume, *Poems Past and Present*, show the lives of individuals controlled by vast abstract concepts: in this they anticipate *The Dynasts*.

He had worked long on the ideas and historical detail out of which this drama grew. In 1891 he referred to his plan for *A Drama of the Times of the First Napoleon*. It was published in three parts in 1904, 1906 and 1908. The central idea Hardy had already explored in the novels and in many poems, namely that Fate is apparently blind and causality haphazard. In his bird's-eye view of the Napoleonic era he presents a universal view of history. We are invited to see what happens when the human individual fails to recognize the Universal Will which operates with regard to society as a whole. The individual will fail to find freedom or happiness until he sees that '*all organic creatures are one family*'. The true realities of life are presented in the drama as spirits or spectral figures. They provide comment on the action and links between the different events. The Spirit of the Pities speaks for loving-kindness; the Spirit of the Years is cold and represents advancement of human knowledge and science. The tragic human individual is the victim of the idiosyncrasies of personal character which usurp human judgment and prevent him from responding to the Immanent Will: Napoleon's downfall is implicit in his character. *The Dynasts* has been staged in extract but Hardy never intended it to be. The scope of the subject and the abstraction of the philosophy work against a unified plot and Hardy shows little stagecraft. In the biography he explains that he wrote it as a poem, not a system of thought.[30]

By now, Hardy was a revered national celebrity. In 1905 he was awarded an Honorary LLD by Aberdeen University. In 1906 he turned down an invitation to attend the dedication of the Carnegie Technical College in Pittsburgh as the guest of the Carnegie Trust. In June 1907 he attended King Edward's garden party at Windsor, and in 1908 he completed an edition of the poems of William Barnes and was elected President-elect of The Society of Dorset Men in London. In 1909 he succeeded Meredith as President of the Society of Authors, was elected a governor of Dorchester Grammar School and attended the first performance of the opera *Tess* (by d'Erlanger) at Covent Garden. More honours came in 1910 with the Order of Merit in June and the freedom of the town of Dorchester in September. His speech in Dorchester was characteristic. Reminding his audience of the town's antiquity, he recalled the Dorchester of his youth: hangings, the stocks, soldiers marching through the town to war, Free Trade riots and the shops. He criticized destruction of some of the old buildings and warned them to preserve what is beautiful. The future of the town he saw as residential with its proximity to the sea, and dry location. He continued:

> *Dorchester's future will not be like its past ; we may be sure of that. Like all other provincial towns, it will lose its individuality — has lost much of it already. We have become almost a London suburb owing to the quickened locomotion, and though some of us may regret this, it has to be.*[31]

The new Wessex edition of the novels occupied much of his time in 1911 and 1912. He received the Gold Medal of the Royal Society of Literature on 1 June; Henry Newbolt and W. B. Yeats came down to Max Gate to present it to him. Rather abruptly in November his wife Emma caught a chill and died. Their relationship had not improved substantially and the flood of grief released by her death is extraordinary. Precise memories of the days of their courtship returned to him, many of them recorded in the sequence of poems 'Veteris Vestigia Flammae'. The poems express the love which he had, at base, always had for his wife, and his great regret that he had not done more to bridge the distance that had separated them latterly:

> *Why, then, latterly did we not speak,*
> *Did we not think of those days long dead,*
> *And ere your vanishing strive to seek*
> *That time's renewal? We might have said,*
> > *'In this bright spring weather*
> > *We'll visit together*
> *Those places that once we visited.'*

> *Well, well! All's past amend,*
> *Unchangeable. It must go.*
> *I seem but a dead man held on end*
> *To sing down soon.... O you could not know*
> > *That such swift fleeing*
> > *No soul foreseeing —*
> *Not even I — would undo me so!*[32]

He made such a pilgrimage to St Juliot's the following year, forty-three years after his first journey there as a young architect.

RE-MARRIAGE AND HIS LAST FOURTEEN YEARS (1913–28)

In June 1913, he visited Cambridge to receive an Honorary Doctorate. He was made an Honorary Fellow of Magdalene College in the same year. In February 1914, in the unforgettable words of his second wife and biographer, *'the subject of this memoir married the present writer'*. Florence Dugdale (1879–1937) had known Hardy for several years. She had undertaken secretarial tasks for him, and when Emma died she made herself as helpful as she could. They had known each other romantically for some years and marriage seemed logical, though, as Dr Gittings has shown, Hardy treated her little better than Emma. Typing out love poems about Emma and other women and preparing the material for an autobiography (that she was later to alter so as to denigrate Hardy's portrait of his first wife) must have caused Florence some pain. After his second marriage Hardy continued to correspond and fall in love with a series of other women. Like Eustacia Vye, Hardy seems to have been constantly in love with the distant and unobtainable.

The war of 1914–18 finally destroyed any belief he had left of man's capacity for self-enoblement. His curious mixture of pessimism and conventionality is seen in three diary entries in 1919. They had celebrated his birthday with a visit to Salisbury Cathedral where he called on the Bishop who, by a curious coincidence, had chosen that day to visit Hardy in Dorchester. Three weeks later he was writing to the Bishop of Durham, one of the Moule family whom he had known as a boy. The letter starts:

> *You may agree with me in thinking it a curious coincidence that the evening before your letter . . . we were reading a chapter in Job etc.*

And yet, between the two events, we find this respectable, Bible-reading friend of bishops writing, in a reply to Mrs Henniker's birthday letter:

> *. . . so why does not Christianity throw up the sponge and say, I am beaten, and let another religion take its place?*[33]

In his Preface to *Late Lyrics and Earlier* (1921) he expresses a desire to rationalize the Anglican Church to embrace the majority of thinkers who had lost their faith in the supernatural. The 1925 version of the Book of Common Prayer proved to him that this was impossible.

In the period between his remarriage and his death he seldom moved from Max Gate, where he was visited by many famous people as well as several young authors. In a hired car he renewed his acquaintance with the countryside, taking tea in one of the many inns he loved. His brother Henry lived at Talbothays and they saw each other often.

More honours were heaped on him. He went in person to receive an Honorary Degree from Oxford (he had succeeded where Jude had failed) and later in the year he was made Honorary Fellow of Queens' College. His visit to Oxford, where he had seen a production of *The Dynasts*, was popular with the undergraduates, and in several subsequent years the Hardys were delighted to play host to the Balliol Players who performed a Greek play at Max Gate on his birthday.

Hardy continued to write up to the end of 1927. His final book of poems, *Winter Words*, had been completed that year and he now found his strength failing. He died early in 1928. His body was buried in Poets' Corner, Westminster Abbey, but his heart lies in Stinsford churchyard between the graves of his two wives.

Three very different houses which Hardy lived in at three stages of his life tell us a lot about him. The house at Max Gate, Dorchester, built to his own design in 1885, is solid and Victorian. It is the house of a man who is now famous. It speaks to us of social respectability and financial success, a place in which you could entertain the Balliol Players or the Prince of Wales. Yet, when Hardy died in 1928, it was a little old-fashioned: it had no bath and was bitterly cold in winter.

In 1876 Hardy was a young, popular author as a result of the success of *Far from the Madding Crowd*, but he was not yet rich. The house which he and Emma found at Sturminster Newton stretched their financial resources. The front of the house, reached by a short driveway, overlooks the River Stour immediately below. To the left a water-meadow stretches to the old water-mill and beyond that is Sturminster Bridge. It is associated with one of the happiest phases of his life, his recent professional success and the intense happiness of his early married life with Emma.

Max Gate, 1900

Riverside Villa, Sturminster Newton, 1876

The Hardy family cottage at Higher Bockhampton

The thatched cottage at the end of Veterans' Valley at Higher Bockhampton is of a different century, a different class and a different way of life. It is not hard to imagine Hardy sitting on the ledge of the window of his bedroom under the eaves, where as a boy he read or did homework and where as a young man he wrote *Under the Greenwood Tree* and *Far from the Madding Crowd*. He has described this cottage so often. It is Mrs Yeobright's house in *The Return of the Native*, where Eustacia played the part of the Turkish Knight in the Christmas mummers' play. It is the tranter's cottage in *Under the Greenwood Tree*. It also appears in the poems 'The Self-Unseeing' and 'Domicilium'[34]:

It faces west, and round the back and sides
High beeches, bending, hang a veil of boughs,
And sweep against the roof. Wild honeysucks
Climb on the walls, and seem to sprout a wish
(If we may fancy wish of trees and plants)
To overtop the apple-trees hard by.

Red roses, lilacs, variegated box
Are there in plenty, and such hardy flowers
As flourish best untrained. Adjoining these
Are herbs and esculents; and farther still
A field; then cottages with trees, and last
The distant hills and sky.

Behind, the scene is wilder. Heath and furze
Are everything that seems to grow and thrive
Upon the uneven ground. A stunted thorn
Stands here and there, indeed; and from a pit
An oak uprises, springing from a seed
Dropped by some bird a hundred years ago.

                    In days bygone—
Long gone—my father's mother, who is now
Blest with the blest, would take me out to walk.
At such a time I once inquired of her
How looked the spot when first she settled here.
The answer I remember. 'Fifty years
Have passed since then, my child, and change has marked
The face of all things. Yonder garden-plots
And orchards were uncultivated slopes
O'ergrown with bramble bushes, furze and thorn:
That road a narrow path shut in by ferns,
Which, almost trees, obscured the passer-by.
Our house stood quite alone, and those tall firs
And beeches were not planted. Snakes and efts
Swarmed in the summer days, and nightly bats
Would fly about our bedrooms. Heathcroppers
Lived on the hills, and were our only friends;
So wild it was when first we settled here.'

The cottage holds continuity between the past and the present,
expressed in the different generations and the oak springing from

Thomas Hardy, O. M. by Augustus John (Reproduced by permission of the Syndics of the Fitzwilliam Museum, Cambridge)

the seed dropped by a bird a hundred years ago. This feeling is absent from Max Gate; but, although in some respects Hardy in his own life followed the process of alienation from the natural environment that he records in his work, there is continuity in the figure of Hardy himself. Thomas Hardy, O.M., surrounded by books in his Max Gate study, is still a countryman. A liking for routine, carefulness about money, awareness of minute natural detail, an ear for the richness of country speech, a wry acceptance of the ironies and tragedies of life and a capacity for regular hard work: not all countrymen have them, but they are country virtues that Hardy had learnt in his youth. He retained them till his death at the age of 87.

N.B. All references to Hardy's novels are to the Macmillan Students' Hardy editions (Macmillan, 1975).

[1] J. Gibson *Thomas Hardy: The Complete Poems* (Macmillan, 1976) 822 'To Louisa in the Lane'; Florence E. Hardy *The Life of Thomas Hardy* (Macmillan, 1966) pp. 26 and 219 [2] as 1 (Gibson), 1 'Domicilium' [3] *ibid.* 9 'Neutral Tones' [4] R. Gittings *Young Thomas Hardy* (Heinemann, 1975) pp. 92–94 [5] *ibid.* p. 109 [6] as 1 (Gibson), 38 'Thoughts of Phena'; as 1 (Hardy), p. 224 [7] Thomas Hardy *Under the Greenwood Tree* Bk. 1 Chap. 7 and Bk. 4 Chap. 1 [8] as 1 (Gibson), 680 'At Rushy Pond' and 827 'The Mound' [9] L. Deacon and T. Coleman *Providence and Mr Hardy* (Hutchinson, 1966) [10] as 4, pp. 223–229 [11] as 1 (Gibson), 874 'Standing by the Mantlepiece'; as 4, p. 181 [12] as 1 (Hardy), p. 111 [13] *ibid.* p. 118 [14] *ibid.* p. 116 [15] Thomas Hardy *Tess of the d'Urbervilles* Chap. 14 [16] Thomas Hardy *Jude the Obscure* Bk. 5 Chaps. 3–7 and Bk. 6 Chaps. 1–2 [17] as 1 (Gibson), 425 'The Musical Box' [18] *ibid.* 426 'On Sturminster Bridge' [19] as 1 (Hardy), p. 148 [20] *ibid.* p. 139 [21] *ibid.* p. 205; H. Orel *Thomas Hardy: Personal Writings* (Macmillan, 1967) pp. 175–176 [22] J. S. Cox (Ed.) *Monographs on the Life, Times and Works of Thomas Hardy: No. 65, 1970—Cook at Max Gate by Annie Mitchell* (Toucan Press, 1970) p. 398 [23] as 1 (Hardy), p. 215 [24] *ibid.* p. 224 [25] William Shakespeare *King Lear* Act 4, scene 1 [26] as 15, Part 6 Chap. 45 p. 425 [27] as 1 (Hardy), p. 246 [28] L. Johnson *The Art of Thomas Hardy* (John Lane, 1923) [29] as 1 (Hardy), p. 272 [30] *ibid.* p. 335 [31] *ibid.* p. 353 [32] as 1 (Gibson), 277 'The Going' verse 5, line 6 [33] as 1 (Hardy), pp. 388–390 [34] as 1 (Gibson), 135 'The Self-Unseeing' and 1 'Domicilium'.

2

Rural Dorset in the Nineteenth Century

INTRODUCTORY: THE NOVELIST AND THE CRITIC AND THE SOCIAL HISTORIAN

Thomas Hardy, the novelist, is only incidentally a social historian. The distinction, irrelevant in considering most novelists, becomes important in the study of one whose fiction provides a social portrait of his age that is fuller, broader and more informative than we find in the accounts of historians. The historian must work from evidenced data, which he then tries to interpret. The novelist is not confined in this way and his intentions are different. He will draw on his own experience and knowledge in creating them, but his plot, his characters and his settings are fictional. Not only may he manipulate them at will but he may use them symbolically or ironically in a way understood only in the context of the novel. Extracting items of social history from Hardy's work and interpreting them, we run the risk of losing sight of their relation to the work as a whole. In Hardy criticism, this has led to critical interpretations as widely differing as those of Douglas Brown[1] and Merryn Williams[2]. The one charts Hardy's lament for the collapse of the small, organic, rural community; the other shows Hardy's portrait of the class tensions and exploitation of labour in a society moving from medieval dependence towards capitalism. Both are fine studies but somehow the emphasis of the critic has in each case obscured the ambiguity of the actual novels. In any study of the authenticity of Hardy's portrait of his age in rural Dorset we must resist constructing a cult figure of the author that reflects our special interests.

RURAL SOCIETY IN THE NINETEENTH
CENTURY: AN HISTORICAL SURVEY
1. THE ENGLISH AGRICULTURAL LABOURER

The central fact of English social history in the nineteenth century is the vast increase of population. By 1801 the population of Great Britain had grown to ten and a half millions, much of it to be found in the developing industrial areas of the North and the Midlands. Between 1801 and 1851 the population nearly doubled, and between 1851 and 1911 it more than re-doubled. The two most obvious requirements of such an expanded population were food and jobs.

He whose labour grew the food that fed the nation was the worst paid, and the worst paid agricultural labourers were in Dorset, where there was no competition for their labour from industry. In 1837 the Dorset labourer earned seven shillings and sixpence a week, whilst his Cheshire counterpart received thirteen shillings a week. In Joseph Arch's words:

> *About the time of the Repeal* [of the Corn Laws in 1846] *things had got so bad that they could hardly be worse. The food we could get was of very poor quality and there was too little of it. Meat was rarely, if ever, seen on the labourer's table. The price was too high for his pocket.... In many a household even a morsel of bacon was considered a great luxury. Flour was so dear that the cottage loaf was mostly of barley. Tea ran to six and seven shillings a pound, sugar would be eightpence a pound, and the price of other provisions was in proportion.... With corn at a prohibitive price, with fresh meat hardly ever within their reach, with what potatoes there were hoarded up and not for the buying — what in the name of necessity were the people to do?*[3]

The trade union leader is writing of his childhood in Burford, Warwickshire. In Dorset it was worse. The year 1830 saw a march on London of impoverished agricultural labourers from all over the south of England from Kent to Dorset. They demanded higher wages and higher rates of poor relief. As a result nine men were hanged and four hundred and fifty-seven were transported. In a letter to Rider Haggard, Hardy writes of the Dorset labourer:

... down to 1850 and 1855 his condition was in general one of the greatest hardship. . . . As a child I knew by sight a sheep-keeping boy who, to my horror, shortly afterwards died of want, the contents of his stomach at the autopsy being raw turnip only.[4]

The employment of labourers was controlled by the hiring fairs of market towns, like those described in chapter six of *Far from the Madding Crowd* and chapters twenty-three and twenty-four of *The Mayor of Casterbridge*, held in Dorchester on 14 February. The real income of a family would depend on the number of working members. Arch notes that *'homeliving boys, aged 12 to 18 were a great asset'* and that *'wives of other families had to work in the fields'*. As late as 1867 a Royal Commission reported that children younger than six were working in the fields of Dorset.

A Dorset agricultural labourer, around 1900 (Dorset County Library)

Ill health or old age could lose the labourer his job and his tied cottage. The alternatives were penury and immurement, separated from wife and family, in the hated Union Workhouse, established under the Poor Law Amendment Act of 1834. In the same year, six labourers from the village of Tolpuddle, not four miles from Hardy's birthplace, were transported for attempting to form a trade union. The recent musical documentary play, *The Wellesbourne Tree*, traces the story of Joseph Arch and the foundation of the National Agricultural Labourers' Union in 1872.[5]

This is the class from which Jemima Hardy had escaped. Her father had died young, and she was brought up on poor relief. Born in 1840, Thomas Hardy's attitudes to the fate of the poor must have been formed as much from what he was told at his mother's knee as from his own observation of contemporary suffering. In Jemima's experience of poverty in the 1820s and 1830s we may find the origin of Hardy's constant preoccupation with the attainment of social and financial standing as well as with the fate of those who sank into penury. The ambiguity of his attitude to those in his novels who attempt to rise above their fate is a subject to which I shall return later.

2. FLUCTUATIONS IN BRITISH AGRICULTURE (1815–1902)

The fluctuations of the wheat trade provide a barometer of the state of British agriculture during the century. Dorset had a mixed arable-livestock agriculture and so felt some of the changes less violently than some other counties; but the labourer felt it, for, deprived of wheat, he was without the staple of a poor man's diet, bread.

During the Napoleonic Wars, a government bounty had encouraged the growing of wheat, but the increased acreage could not match increased needs. The Corn Laws of 1815 were designed to prohibit foreign corn and stimulate home growth by placing a heavy tariff on imported corn. In fact this benefited nobody. The increased price of home corn was not sufficient to protect the investment of those farmers who had increased their acreage and the poor simply could not afford it. Attempts to introduce a sliding scale of tariffs were equally unsuccessful. The Anti-Corn Law League, founded by Cobden and Bright in 1839, strove to abolish the tariff altogether. A series of poor harvests culminating in the failure of the Irish potato crop in 1845 forced the hand of Peel's Government, and in 1846 the Corn Laws were at last repealed, allowing cheap European and American corn into the country. Since America needed the consumer products produced in Britain's new factories, the consequent trade exchange gave a considerable boost to the economy.

That at least is the judgment of historians, a long-term, dispassionate, economic assessment. But the poverty of the agricultural labourer, the inflated price of basic foods and the misery that has always accompanied widespread unemployment were close facts to Hardy during his childhood. Historians have called the time that followed the Repeal of the Corn Laws 'The Golden Age of British Agriculture' (1846–74), and it is true that some of the national factors did benefit Dorset—the coming of the railway in 1847 took local dairy products and Portland stone to the expanding metropolis, and new techniques and mechanized farm machinery became widely available. But we have to ask who benefited from the new markets, who was affected by the new machinery and what happened when farms became more specialized and 'efficient'. We still see around us on any train journey through rural Britain the wealth that farming produced in the middle of the nineteenth century, the large stone farm houses and complexes of farm buildings. But it is in contemporary writing that we see how the times felt from the other end of the class structure. Mechanization of the sort Hardy symbolizes in the threshing machine in *Tess of the d'Urbervilles* brought a new sort of farming, streamlined, on a large scale, and technical. For the farmer there were for a while increased profits; for the enterprising man (like Gabriel Oak in *Far from the Madding Crowd*) there was capital available to start up a concern; but for the labourer there were few benefits. More intensive farming did not create more jobs and the work often became less varied and required only at certain seasons of the year. Whilst his mother's stories of the workhouse and widespread poverty before the Repeal of the Corn Laws surely provide much of Hardy's emotional concern with the plight of the labourer, many of the situations that he describes reflect very truly the problems for Dorset labourers right through and beyond the middle years of the century. Unemployment, being turned out of tied cottages, seasonal labour, new mechanized techniques in farms, new accounting techniques in businesses, gradations and differences between the employers and the employed, the impact of the towns and educated men on the rural scene: these are the realistic situations we meet in the Wessex novels.

Evening in the labourer's cottage (The Mansell Collection)

The so-called Golden Age of British Agriculture ended abruptly with the opening up of the American Prairies in the late 1860s. Combine-harvested cheap grain flooded the British market and undercut home prices, forcing many farmers into bankruptcy. Again it was the farm labourer who had least to shield him from the effects of the two great periods of agricultural depression (1875–84 and 1891–99). Those farmers who had cut their losses and turned arable land into grazing for livestock were thwarted first by outbreaks of foot and mouth disease and liver rot, following the wettest summer on record in 1879; and then the following year saw the first imports of meat from New Zealand, Australia and Argentina in refrigerated steamships at prices with which British farmers could not compete.

Farms folded and labour became scarce. Encouraged by Joseph Arch's Agricultural Labourers' Union, those labourers who could flocked to better job prospects in the cities, or emigrated. The employment of children had been prevented by the introduction of compulsory education (1870) and the Agricultural Children's Act of 1873. In the thirty years 1870–1900, 300,000 agricultural workers left the countryside. Labour on farms became increasingly casual and labour gangs moved from one seasonal employment to another. It is a phenomenon we meet in *Tess* when the dairymaids move on to winter work drawing reeds and grubbing turnips for Farmer Groby at Flintcomb-Ash. Of the exodus from the country villages Hardy comments:

> However, all the mutations so increasingly discernible in village life did not originate entirely in the agricultural unrest. A depopulation was also going on. The village had formerly contained, side by side with the agricultural labourers, an interesting and better-informed class, ranking distinctly above the former—the class to which Tess's father and mother had belonged—and including the carpenter, the smith, the shoemaker, the huckster, together with nondescript workers other than farm-labourers; a set of people who owed a certain stability of aim and conduct to the fact of their being life-holders like Tess's father, or copyholders, or, occasionally, small freeholders. But as the long holdings fell in they were seldom again let to similar tenants, and were mostly pulled down, if not absolutely required by the farmer for his hands. Cottagers who were not directly

employed on the land were looked upon with disfavour, and the banishment of some starved the trade of others, who were thus obliged to follow. These families, who had formed the backbone of the village life in the past, who were the depositaries of the village traditions, had to seek refuge in the large centres; the process, humorously designated by statisticians as 'the tendency of the rural population towards the large towns', being really the tendency of water to flow uphill when forced by machinery.[6]

A summary of the state of agriculture in Dorset at the end of the century appears in the *Victoria County History* of 1908:

So great has been the change that the farmer of 1800, were he alive now, would scarcely recognize this county. The number of sheep kept has dwindled, the corn area has become less, dairying is more general, the area of permanent and rotation pasture has been increased, and many small industries . . . have completely died out.

Not all of Hardy's major Wessex novels are centrally concerned with the collapse of rural culture, but taken as a body they do provide us with a record of what has been displaced. It is with the different aspects of that culture that the next chapter is concerned.

[1] Douglas Brown *Thomas Hardy* (Longmans, 1954) [2] Merryn Williams *Thomas Hardy and Rural England* (Macmillan, 1972) [3] John G. O'Leary (Ed.) *The Autobiography of Joseph Arch* (Macgibbon & Kee, 1966) p. 22 [4] H. R. Haggard *Rural England* (London, 1902) p. 265 [5] Robert Leach *The Wellesbourne Tree* (Blackie, 1975) [6] Thomas Hardy *Tess of the d'Urbervilles* Chap. 51 pp. 485–486.

3

Hardy's Portrait of an Age

WESSEX AND THE SETTINGS OF FOUR NOVELS

Wessex, the setting of most of the novels, must have seemed as distant and fictional to many of Hardy's readers as Tolkien's land of Middle Earth does to us. Hardy's map shows us Wessex stretching westward to Devon and Cornwall; its northern limits are the Bristol Channel to the west and Oxford to the east; and its heart is Dorset and the area around Dorchester that Hardy knew as a child. But this is no fictional land of hobbits. These are actual places with closely observed and surprisingly varied agricultural economies which we follow through the agricultural year. From novel to novel we move to different working communities: from the woodland community around Stinsford to the mixed arable-livestock farms around Puddletown; from the desolate heathland to the east of Bockhampton to the timber and cider country of the Vale of Blackmoor; from the fertile dairy farms of the Frome Valley to a '*starve-acre*' exposed hill-farm on a chalk plateau north-east of Alton Pancras; and there in the centre is the market town of Dorchester, the Casterbridge of the novels. When we examine these settings in each novel we find a distinctive dual function, in one direction towards the sort of authentic detail that creates realism, and in the other towards symbolism. Very few places in the novels exist simply as the place where an incident occurs; invariably a place carries a power of suggestion that links it with the feelings and personalities of the story's characters.

FAR FROM THE MADDING CROWD (1873)

Although Casterbridge, with its Corn Exchange and its Union Workhouse, plays an important part in this novel, the central setting is Bathsheba Everdene's farm at Weatherbury. Most of the monthly episodes focus on one or two closely described events on or about the farm. In the farmhouse itself, described at the beginning of chapter nine, Bathsheba meets her farm labourers for the first time; from it she sends the fateful valentine; half-in and half-out of it mistress and men celebrate the sheep-shearing, and in the middle of a sitting-room next to the hall is laid the coffin of '*Fanny Robin and child*'. Unlike Boldwood's house which, rather like him, is grave and austere but with a roaring fire at its centre (chapter fourteen), Bathsheba's farmhouse is full of twists and restless creaks (chapter nine). Outside in the stackyard stand ricks of straw and, on stone staddles, of wheat. Gabriel saves them twice in memorable scenes which at once show us his caring relationship to Bathsheba and to the responsibilities of farming. The fire and storm also symbolically enact the torrent of Gabriel's feelings, yet each description is meticulous in its realism.

Bathsheba's Great Tithe Barn is modelled on the one in Cerne Abbas and Hardy makes it quite clear what it represents: a harmony between man and his labour which is as old as farming and workfolk.

> *Five decades hardly modified the cut of a gaiter, the embroidery of a smock-frock, by the breadth of a hair. Ten generations failed to alter the turn of a single phrase. In these Wessex nooks the busy outsider's ancient times are only old; his old times are still new; his present is futurity.*
>
> *So the barn was natural to the shearers, and the shearers were in harmony with the barn.*[1]

Troy, with his irresponsibility and ignorance, destroys that harmony when he threatens his workfolk with dismissal if they do not stay and get drunk with him in that same barn on the occasion of the harvest supper, while outside the storm threatens the unprotected ricks.

The farm is mixed arable-livestock. Some Devon red cattle are mentioned and the farmyard hens, but naturally more prominent is Gabriel Oak's work as a shepherd. In the winter we see him bringing the early lambs down to the warm malthouse for weaning. At the end of May (chapter nineteen) the sheep are dipped as two cuckoos sing from a knot of foliage and Bathsheba turns towards Boldwood. She quarrels with Gabriel as he grinds the shears for the shearing but within twenty-four hours she has recalled him to pierce the swollen sheep who have become blasted on clover. By June at the sheep-shearing he cannot conceal his jealous irritation and carelessly nicks a sheep when Boldwood appears. On the night of the shearing supper Bathsheba turns from Oak to Boldwood and promises that she will give him an answer to his proposal by harvest; ironically, later the same evening she meets the dashing Sergeant Troy who is to win her love. Bathsheba's disregard for Gabriel's feelings is echoed in Coggan's song, *'I've lost my love, and I care not'*.

At the height of summer, an irresistible natural force is seen equally in the settings and in Troy and Bathsheba's mutual attraction. The sword-drill at Maiden Castle is often cited, but equally suggestive of nature's fecundity are the hay harvest, when Troy presses his attentions on Bathsheba, and the hiving of the swarm of bees which he takes over from her. But Troy lacks constancy, and when fire and the storm threaten Bathsheba's livelihood which is invested in the harvest it is Oak who saves them. This contrast between Troy and Oak is again made when Cainy Ball returns from Bath and tells the men getting in the oat harvest that he has seen Troy with Bathsheba. Whereas Gabriel is seen so many times working the farm with skill, patience and understanding, Troy ignores it and squanders Bathsheba's capital. Troy's inability to enter into a constant and purposeful relationship with either Fanny or Bathsheba finds its parallel in his failure to manage the farm.

Warren's Malthouse, the meeting place of Bathsheba's labourers, is important to the plot on three occasions. Sitting round the fire with their cider, the rustics provide information, comment and a good deal of yokel humour which verges on caricature. But the impact of these scenes is something more subtle. It rests partly on the ease of the working relationship of the men who meet there, partly on the convivial drinking and eating that occurs there, partly on their humour and simplicity and partly on a feeling of continuity between past and present that the scenes represent. Rightness of relationship to people and to environment, expressed in Warren's Malthouse, is again felt in Hardy's description of the Great Barn, in Gabriel Oak telling the time from the stars, playing his flute or tending his flock on Norcombe Hill, and in the picture of married life he expresses to Bathsheba:

> *'And at home by the fire, whenever you look up, there I shall be—and whenever I look up, there will be you.'*[2]

In fact, this general impression of Warren's Malthouse is

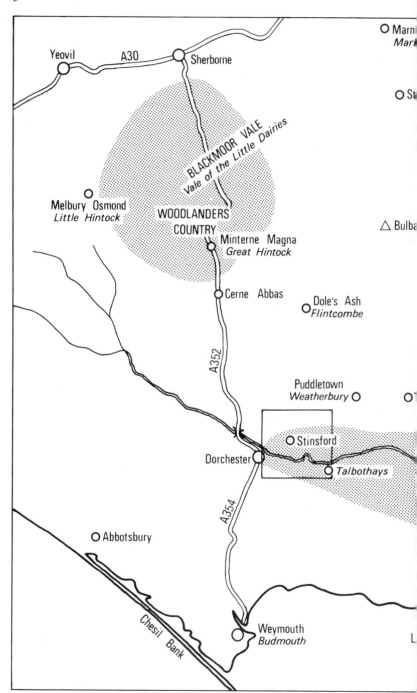

Map of the area around Dorchester in which most of the Wessex novels are set

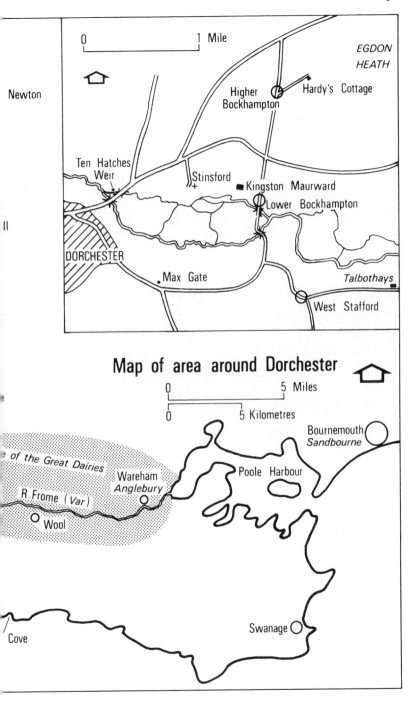

Map of area around Dorchester

'Rightness of relationship to people and environment': a shepherd with his dogs (copyright, The Toucan Press)

produced as much from the little realistic details as from the conversation. The three-legged table at which the maltster has his bacon and bread, the potatoes roasting in the ash pit, Henery's drab kerseymere coat, the lanterns which he blows out as the dawn comes through the one pane of glass and the two-handled God-forgive-me cider cup from which they drink: these familiar details are described with much affection, and they suggest a warmth and intimacy with the immediate environment that is lacking from the houses of Bathsheba and Boldwood.

THE WOODLANDERS (1879)

To the north of Dorchester lie the North Dorset Downs. The A 352 follows the valley of the River Cerne through the Downs to Cerne Abbas, and between Cerne and Sherborne, some eight miles further north, is Woodlanders country. Three miles beyond Cerne you come to the crest of a hill at Dogbury Gate. Ahead lies the Vale of Blackmore, High Stoy on the left and Dogbury Hill to the right. In the 1912 Preface Hardy tells us that the story is set in the wooded land overlooked from High Stoy. Melbury Osmond is the original for Great Hintock; Little Hintock is imaginary. Mrs Charmond's house was modelled on Turnworth House near Sturminster Newton (no longer standing), and Sherton Abbas is Sherborne. The Earl of Wessex Hotel where Giles set up his cider press may be found in Digby Street but is now a boarding house for Sherborne school. The market-place where he stood beneath the sample apple tree tied to his waggon is in Cheap Street:

> . . . *the boughs rose above the heads of the farmers, and brought a delightful suggestion of orchards into the heart of the town.*

The novel starts with an intrusion into Little Hintock, that of Barber Percombe who has come to buy Marty South's fine locks of hair to make into a wig for Mrs Charmond. Many, though by no means all, of the tragic events of the story can be attributed to other intrusions into the calm, bucolic life of the village. Mrs Charmond returns from abroad. Fitzpiers moves into the area, bringing with him new medical and philosophical ideas. The boarding-school education that Grace has received outside the area makes her blind to Giles's qualities and leads her into an unhappy marriage.

The life intruded upon is one of close intimacy with the woodland, gained through working on it. John South has this affinity and dies when the tree outside his window is felled. We see it in Giles Winterborne as he plants the trees:

> *Although he would seem to shovel in the earth quite carelessly there was a sort of sympathy between himself and the fir, oak, or beech that he was operating on; so that the roots took hold of the soil in a few days.*[3]

Winterborne has a similar reciprocity with Marty South who follows behind him as he plants, filling in with soil:

> *They had planted together, and together they had felled; together they had, with the run of the years, mentally*

> *collected those remoter signs and symbols which seen in few were of runic obscurity, but all together made an alphabet.*[4]

This sort of unwritten knowledge is something different from book-learning (like Fitzpiers's) or schooling (like Grace's). It is also to be found in the relationship between Giles and Melbury at the novel's start:

> *For this reason a curious kind of partnership existed between Melbury and the younger man—a partnership based upon an unwritten code, by which each acted in the way he thought fair towards the other, on a give-and-take principle. Melbury, with his timber and copse-ware business, found that the weight of his labour came in winter and spring. Winterborne was in the apple and cider trade, and his requirements in cartage and other work came in the autumn of each year. Hence horses, waggons, and in some degree men, were handed over to him when the apples began to fall; he, in return, lending his assistance to Melbury in the busiest wood-cutting season, as now.*[5]

This world of work is descibed with great precision and affection. An early scene is of Marty cutting spar gads by lantern light. She takes them to Melbury's waggon house where there are four huge waggons

> *built on those ancient lines whose proportions have been ousted by modern patterns. . . . One was laden with sheep cribs, another with hurdles, another with ash poles, and the fourth, at the foot of which she had placed her thatching-spars, was half full of similar bundles.*[6]

In the next chapter there is similar exactitude in the description of Melbury's square yard or quadrangle,

> *formerly a regular carriage entrance, though the middle of the area was now made use of for stacking timber, faggots, hurdles, and other products of the wood. . . . The building on the left . . . was a long-backed erection, now used for spar-making, sawing, crib-framing, and copse-ware manufacture in general.*[7]

The occupants of the yard are

> *John Upjohn, Melbury's regular man; a neighbour engaged in the hollow-turnery trade; old Timothy Tangs and young Timothy Tangs, top and bottom sawyers at work in Mr. Melbury's pit outside; Farmer Cawtree, who kept the cider-house, and Robert Creedle, an old man who worked for Winterborne.*[8]

We see different aspects of Giles's work: delivering timber for Melbury, selling cider trees in Sherton market-place, planting trees, and, in autumn, processing apples with his portable cider press which he has set up outside the Earl of Wessex Hotel.

> *He looked and smelt like Autumn's very brother, his face being sunburnt to wheat-colour, his eyes blue as cornflowers, his sleeves and leggings dyed with fruit-stains, his hands clammy with the sweet juice of apples, his hat sprinkled with pips, and everywhere about him that atmosphere of cider which at its first return each season has such an indescribable fascination for those who have been born and bred among the orchards.*[9]

Even Fitzpiers comes round to some realization that Giles's work is an extension of his character when, seeking out Marty for news of Grace at the end of the novel, he finds her polishing Giles's tools; he promises to buy her Giles's cider press so that she can carry on his work. There is tremendous dignity, simplicity and love in her final words over Giles's grave that end the book, for they assert timeless values of man's relationship to place, work and loved ones, values shown in his life and restated in Marty:

> '*Whenever I plant the young larches I'll think that none can plant as you planted; and whenever I split a gad, and whenever I turn the cider wring, I'll say none could do it like you. If ever I forget your name let me forget home and heaven! ... But no, no my love, I never can forget 'ee; for you was a good man, and did good things!*'[10]

In Marty and Giles we are shown two characters who work in harmony with their environment, but the environment itself is far from being idyllic. Hardy builds up a strong sense of the essential sadness and cruelty of nature. The melancholy opening expresses loneliness and foreshadows death:

> *The physiognomy of a deserted highway expresses solitude to a degree that is not reached by mere dales or downs, and bespeaks a tomb-like stillness more emphatic than that of glades and pools.*[11]

When Marty opens the door of her cottage to deliver her spar gads she hears

> *the creaking sound of two overcrowded branches in the neighbouring wood, which were rubbing each other into wounds, and other vocalized sorrows of the trees . . .*[12]

Natural events are given human qualities. The dawn of that morning is described thus:

> *. . . and presently the bleared white visage of a sunless winter day emerged like a dead-born child. . . . Owls that had been catching mice in the outhouses, rabbits that had been eating the winter-greens in the gardens, and stoats that had been sucking the blood of the rabbits, discerning that their human neighbours were on the move discreetly withdrew from publicity, and were seen and heard no more till nightfall.*[13]

The progression in this chain of nature's predatory violence leads straight to humans. There is a similar affinity between the natural and human worlds in Marty's words as she plants the trees with Giles:

> *'How they sigh directly we pick them up, though while they are lying down they don't sigh at all.'*[14]

The closeness to her own life does not have to be made explicit.

Underlying Hardy's use of cruel nature as a metaphor for human life is his acceptance of Darwin's discovery that nature does not follow a divine plan, but is mindless, cruel and gives survival to the strong. Consider this description of Grace and her father walking through the woods to the timber auction:

> *They went noiselessly over mats of starry moss, rustled through interspersed tracts of leaves, skirted trunks with spreading roots whose mossed rinds made them like hands wearing green gloves; elbowed old elms and ashes with great forks, in which stood pools of water that overflowed on rainy days and ran down their stems in green cascades.*

The world of work in *The Woodlanders*: felling trees in about 1890 (University of Reading, Museum of English Rural Life)

So far, the likeness of trees to men is a gentle and rather magical thing: '*starry moss*' and '*green cascades*' give the mood. But the pretty metaphor develops into something altogether more disturbing:

> *On older trees still than these huge lobes of fungi grew like lungs. Here, as everywhere, the Unfulfilled Intention, which makes life what it is, was as obvious as it could be among*

Hurdle-making, 1895 (copyright, The Toucan Press)

Cider-making, circa 1900. The press is similar to that used by Giles Winterborne. (Mr R. Rogers)

the depraved crowds of a city slum. The leaf was deformed, the curve was crippled, the taper was interrupted; the lichen ate the vigour of the stalk, and the ivy slowly strangled to death the promising sapling.[15]

The unfulfilled love that is the story's dominant theme follows a universal pattern that is as observable in the city slum as it is in nature. Hardy's implication is that the intention of the Creator at the beginning of the world has not been fulfilled: in the cruelty of nature and that of man (whose emblem in the story is the man-trap) Hardy can see no working out of a divine purpose. The pattern that does emerge is of universal suffering. Much later in the story when Giles is lying under hurdles in the wood, dying as a result of Grace's foolish adherence to social convention, the scene that she sees from her window completely echoes their situation:

Above stretched an old beech, with vast arm-pits, and great pocket-holes in its sides where branches had been removed in past times; a black slug was trying to climb it. Dead boughs were scattered about like ichthyosauri in a museum, and beyond them were perishing woodbine stems resembling old ropes.

From the other window all she could see were more trees, in jackets of lichen and stockings of moss. At their roots were stemless yellow fungi like lemons and apricots, and tall fungi with more stem than stool. Next were more trees close together, wrestling for existence, their branches disfigured with wounds resulting from their mutual rubbings and blows. It was the struggle between these neighbours that she had heard in the night.[16]

There is a stylistic confidence here that reaches its fullest expression in *Tess of the d'Urbervilles*: the detail of the novel's setting has become completely one with the emotional state and situation of the characters.

THE MAYOR OF CASTERBRIDGE (1884)

Casterbridge is based closely on Dorchester. The number of moves of house in *The Mayor of Casterbridge* is extraordinary. Susan Henchard, Elizabeth-Jane, Jopp, Lucetta and Henchard all make various moves as a result of their rising or declining fortunes. We have most detail of Lucetta's house, High Place Hall, overlooking the market-place, and of the Mayor's house, number ten, South Street. It is fascinating to build up a detailed portrait of this house from the descriptions in chapters nine, ten, twelve, fourteen, thirty-five, thirty-eight and forty-four. It is an old house, *'faced with red-and-grey brick'* and we get to know it intimately. The same can be said of Casterbridge and as we grow in sympathy for the complex personality of Henchard, so we grow in intimacy and affection for the town, so that at the end of the book we experience his isolation from friends and family also as a physical separation from the town whose economic, social and historical character we have got to know very closely.

Susan and Elizabeth-Jane's first walk up High Street reveals Casterbridge as a farming community:

> *The agricultural and pastoral character of the people upon whom the town depended for its existence was shown by the class of objects displayed in the shop windows. Scythes, reap-hooks, sheep-shears, bill-hooks, spades, mattocks, and hoes at the ironmonger's; bee-hives, butterfirkins, churns, milking stools and pails, hay-rakes, field-flagons, and seed-lips at the cooper's; cart ropes and plough-harness at the saddler's; carts, wheel-barrows, and mill-gear at the wheelwright's and machinist's; horse-embrocations at the chemist's; at the glover's and leather-cutter's, hedging-gloves, thatchers' knee-caps, ploughmen's leggings, villagers' pattens and clogs.*[17]

There is a similar concrete realism in Hardy's description of Henchard's stockyard, of the granary where he fights Farfrae and of the corn-waggons which Abel Whittle must get up at 4 a.m. to drive. The weekly market day brings the local farmers into the town and men from the cider district who stand beneath the apple trees they have brought to sell (chapter twenty-two). Elizabeth-Jane points out the local merchants to Lucetta:

> *'There's Mr. Bulge—he's a wine merchant; there's Benjamin Brownlet—a horse dealer; and Kitson, the pig breeder; and Yopper, the auctioneer; beside maltsters, and millers—and so on.'*[18]

On market day the streets become crowded with the wares of the shopkeepers brought out on to trestles in the street (as

High East Street, Dorchester, as it is today.

happens in Cornhill, Dorchester, to this day); horses are tethered
and pigs penned ready for sale. But before this come

> *the vans of the carriers in and out of Casterbridge, who
> hailed from Mellstock, Weatherbury, The Hintocks, Sher-
> ton Abbas, Kingsbere, Overcombe and many other towns
> and villages round.*[19]

> *Thus Casterbridge was in most respects but the pole, focus
> or nerve end of the surrounding country life . . .*[20]

The town is small enough for everyone to know everyone and
the friendly banter in the pubs is the outward sign of mutual
interdependence. Henchard, though he is a harsh employer to
Whittle, keeps his mother in coal. At harvest time everyone joins
in the task:

> *Nearly the whole town had gone into the fields. The
> Casterbridge populace still retained the primitive habit of
> helping one another in time of need ; and thus, though the corn
> belonged to the farming section of the little community—that
> inhabiting the Durnover quarter—the remainder was no less
> interested in the labour of getting it home.*[21]

Elsewhere the relationship to work is described in less idyllic terms. The gibbous forms of the farmers on market day *'specially represented ready cash'* and when at the Candlemas hiring fair the parsimonious Farfrae saves an old shepherd from being separated from his son his motives are not entirely charitable:

> *'I want a young carter; and perhaps I'll take the old man too—yes, he'll not be very expensive and doubtless he will answer my pairpose somehow.'*[22]

When Farfrae takes over Henchard's corn business he gives the workfolk a shilling a week less, which is a lot when you realize that the average labourer in Dorset then would earn about seven shillings a week.

Henchard's reversals of fortune take him through the various social layers of the town. These are clearly divided into three sections: firstly those with money, such as farmers, professional men and successful business men; then the lesser traders and petty officials of the town, among whom we may number Constables Buzzford and Blowbody; and finally the workfolk and those without work. We see each group in their characteristic places of meeting: the wealthy in the King's Arms, where the banquet is presided over by Henchard in chapter five; the lesser tradesmen in The Mariners' Arms, where Farfrae stays, where the choir of All Saints' Church take their Sunday half-pint after church and where Henchard, after twenty-one years of abstinence, breaks out drinking; and the workfolk and rogues in Peter's Finger in Mixen Lane (now Mill Lane), the slum area at the bottom of town adjacent to the River Frome and the open countryside beyond.

> *Mixen Lane was the Adullam of all the surrounding villages. . . . Rural mechanics too idle to mechanize, rural servants too rebellious to serve, drifted or were forced into Mixen Lane. . . . Vice ran freely in and out certain of the doors of the neighbourhood. . . . Even slaughter had not been altogether unknown here . . . mildewed leaf in the sturdy and flourishing Casterbridge plant . . .*[23]

On the road out of the bottom of town across the marshy fields, two bridges have their differing clientele:

> *There was a marked difference of quality between the personages who haunted the near bridge of brick and the*

> *personages who haunted the far one of stone. Those of lowest*
> *character preferred the former, adjoining the town; they did*
> *not mind the glare of the public eye. . . . Their hands were*
> *mostly kept in their pockets; they wore a leather strap*
> *round their hips or knees, and boots that required a deal of*
> *lacing, but seemed never to get any. . . .*
>
>   *The* misérables *who would pause on the remoter bridge*
> *were of a politer stamp. They included bankrupts,*
> *hypochondriacs, persons who were what is called 'out of a*
> *situation' from fault or lucklessness, the inefficient of the*
> *professional class—shabby-genteel men, who did not know*
> *how to get rid of the weary time between breakfast and*
> *dinner and the yet more weary time between dinner and*
> *dark.*[24]

The approximate date of the story's setting is given to us in a
note in Hardy's Preface, in which he draws attention to the
significance of the success of the home corn harvest in the days
just before the Corn Laws of 1846. This was a time when
fortunes could be made rapidly and rapidly lost; in agriculture a
time of flux and transition. Farfrae's new methods of accounting
and book-keeping replace Henchard's slipshod customs; the new
horse drill he demonstrates in the market-place is indicative of
new techniques of mechanized farming. The railway that brings the
Royal personage to Casterbridge in fact reached Dorchester in 1847.
However, it is clear that there was a general lack of prosperity:

> *Prices were like the roads of the period, steep in gradient,*
> *reflecting in their phases the local conditions, without*
> *engineering, levellings, or averages.*
>
>   *The farmer's income was ruled by the wheat-crop within*
> *his own horizon, and the wheat-crop by the weather. . . .*
>
>   *Instead of new articles in the shop-windows, those that*
> *had been rejected in the foregoing summer were brought out*
> *again; superseded reap-hooks, badly-shaped rakes, shop-*
> *worn leggings, and time-stiffened water-tights reappeared,*
> *furbished up as near to new as possible.*[25]

The wealth of historical detail about the town that Hardy
introduces is invariably rather sinister. Hang Fair, held whenever
there was an execution at the County Jail, is referred to twice:

> *. . . at executions the waiting crowd stood in a meadow immediately before the drop, out of which the cows had been temporarily driven to give the spectators room.*[26]

Public execution was abolished only in 1868 and Hardy witnessed two executions in his youth. It is a subject he returns to often in his work with macabre relish. The Bloody Assizes and subsequent hangings on Gallows Hill following Monmouth's Rebellion (1685) are also mentioned.[27]

Over the side door of High Place Hall is a chipped, leering mask which suggests intrigue *'appertaining to the mansion's past history'*.

> *By the alley it had been possible to come unseen from all sorts of quarters of the town—the old play-house, the old bull-stake, the old cock-pit, the pool wherein nameless infants had been used to disappear.*[28]

The *'bull-stake'* referred to stood in the cattle market and was used to secure oxen while they were baited by dogs in order to tenderize the meat before slaughter. And *'in a nearby corner of the cattle market stood the stocks'*.[29]

That Casterbridge is a Roman town gives Hardy further opportunity for doleful detail. Mrs Henchard is buried in the old Roman cemetery where her dust *'mingled with the dust of women who lay ornamented with glass hair pins and amber necklaces, and men who held in their mouths coins of Hadrian, Postumus and the Constantines'*. The unearthing of a buried Roman *'lying on his side, in an oval scoop in the chalk, like a chicken in its shell, his knees drawn up to his chest'* was a frequent occurrence and a familiar spectacle, we are told, to Casterbridge street boys and men.[30] The Ring, *'one of the finest Roman Amphitheatres, if not the very finest, remaining in Britain'* is the melancholy trysting place of Henchard and his wife. Hardy dwells on its gladiatorial associations and a more recent but equally bloody public execution:

> *. . . in 1705 a woman who had murdered her husband was half-strangled and then burnt there in the presence of ten thousand spectators. Tradition reports that at a certain stage of the burning her heart burst and leapt out of her body, to the terror of them all, and that not one of those ten thousand people ever cared particularly for hot roast after that.*[31]

About twenty yards from the Hangman's Cottage lies '*the pool wherein nameless infants had been used to disappear*'

Maumbury Ring, where Mary Channing was burnt to death in 1705

Sinister detail in *The Mayor of Casterbridge*: a recently excavated late Romano-British burial from Poundbury, Dorchester (photograph: Christopher Green)

Hardy exceeds the bounds of good taste and historical accuracy here. The burning took place, but there is no evidence that the unfortunate victim was burnt alive: it was the practice to strangle victims completely before burning them.

One might be tempted to think that these historical perspectives on Casterbridge are introduced simply because of Hardy's antiquarian interests or because of their melodramatic impact. Their function is, I think, more complex. In these references we look back on the history of the town and see instance after instance of cruelty and suffering. Life and death are seen to treat man with a studied indifference. Henchard's own tragedy and death is seen against this perspective. At one point he cannot help thinking

> *that the concatenation of events this evening had produced was the scheme of some sinister intelligence bent on punishing him.*[32]

It is a view of life we meet frequently in Hardy's work.

TESS OF THE D'URBERVILLES (1891)

The misfortunes of Tess are hardly credible outside Victorian melodrama or the ballad sheets. This victim of rape, this mother of an unbaptized child who lives in sin and then murders her lover: are we really expected to see her as the '*Pure Woman*' of the sub-title? That we are and that we do is attributable in large part to the authenticity of Hardy's feelings for his heroine and the strong realism in his telling of her story.

He sets her home in Marlott (Marnhull), a village about one mile from where the newly wedded Hardys lived at Sturminster Newton. Talbothays, the dairy farm by the River Froom in the Valley of the Great Dairies, is the actual farm of that name that was owned by Hardy's father just beyond West Stafford to the east of Dorchester. The farm had been kept by Mr and Mrs Crick and Hardy must have known it well as a boy. Wellbridge Manor is in fact Woolbridge Manor at Wool, and just beyond it at Bindon Abbey can be seen the stone coffin which suggested to Hardy the sleep-walking scene. The Turberville window is in the South wall of Kingsbere church (Bere Regis in the novel) and near it is the entrance to the Turberville vault. Trantridge is probably Pentridge; The Chase is Cranborne Chase; Melchester is Salisbury; Wintonchester is Winchester, and to this day Stonehenge still has a sacrificial altar struck by the rays of the rising sun on Midsummer morning. The literary hiker may follow the route Tess took and, more recently, television cameras have followed from Flintcomb-Ash across the chalk hills north of Dorchester to Evershot (Evershead) and Beaminster (Emminster, where Angel Clare's father was Vicar). Hardy has placed his settings with great exactitude but he denies that '*the fictitious places* 'are' *such and such real ones but are merely places suggested by them*'.

It is the domestic detail rather than the topographical detail that convinces the reader; detail, for example, of the life of Tess's father, a haggler (i.e., a man who lives by buying and selling bargains) who is prone equally to drink, flattery and indolence. Tess is forced to take the load of beehives to Casterbridge market, starting at two o'clock a.m., while her father sleeps off the effects of Mrs Rolliver's strong ale. When the horse, Prince, dies in the accident and the family source of income is lost, she then feels obliged to seek help from the d'Urbervilles. Against her inclination, she goes out of a sense of obligation to her parents. Compare this with the levity of her mother's attitude to Alec's advances: '*And if he don't marry her afore, he will after.*'

Tess is already old enough to resent her mother's improvidence:

> *As Tess grew older, and began to see how matters stood, she felt quite a Malthusian towards her mother for thoughtlessly giving her so many little sisters and brothers, when it was such a trouble to nurse and provide for them.*[33]

Whereas Tess gets things done and copes, both of her parents leave things to Providence. One of the examples of this is when her father dies and they have to move from the lifehold home '*long . . . coveted by the tenant-farmer for his regular labourers*', and Tess takes charge and organizes the move. In this she is the antithesis of Alec d'Urberville who fails to help his mother run Trantridge and then, when she dies, is so upset that he is driven into a skin-deep religious conversion. It is typical of Tess's pragmatism that when her father is ill she tidies up his allotment.

Talbothays is altogether different in feeling. The beauty of the setting combines with the pleasant and productive life of the dairy farm to provide the idyllic background to the courtship of Tess and Angel. It is a one hundred cow dairy farm run by Dairyman Crick and his homely wife who cooks for all the workers. The life of the farm is described in some detail. Tess arrives at about 4.30 p.m. as the dairymen are getting in the red and white cows for milking, and she sees them being milked in the barton in the evening sun. She notices the pattens of the maids '*to keep their shoes above the mulch of the barn*', the turned-down hat brims of the men, and the long, white '*pinner*' of Dairyman Crick. She sleeps in the dairy house,

> *a large room over the milk house some thirty feet long; the sleeping-cots of the other three indoor milkmaids being in the same apartment.*[34]

From the adjacent cheese loft comes the smell of the cheeses, and in the immense attic above, reached by a ladder from the cheese loft, sleeps the romantic agricultural student, Angel Clare.

The atmosphere that hangs over the farm is one of abundant fullness and fruition: the milk oozes from the udders of the cows as they wait in the yard to be milked; the whey drips from the cheese-wrings in the dairy, and pollen bursts from the weeds in the ground, damp and rank with juicy grass, on the outskirts of the garden as Tess is drawn towards the sound of Angel's harp.

> *The floating pollen seemed to be his notes made visible, and the dampness of the garden the weeping of the garden's sensibility.*[35]

Tess, captivated like a bird, and Angel merge into their natural surroundings:

> *Though near nightfall, the rank-smelling weed-flowers glowed as if they would not close for intentness, and the waves of colour mixed with the waves of sound.*[36]

> *Amid the oozing fatness and warm ferments of the Froom Vale, at a season when the rush of juices could almost be heard below the hiss of fertilization, it was impossible that the most fanciful love should not grow passionate.*[37]

Clare is learning the skills of the farm and he meets Tess constantly about her work: in the meadow as they scan it for the garlic that has given the butter a twang; skimming milk in the dairy; breaking up the masses of curd before putting them in the vat; milking in the meadow and, towards the end of the season, driving the milk to the station in the spring waggon. When declining autumn comes with the early days of October they wander together by the banks of the Var (or Froom).

The idyllic setting also contains the suggestion of later unhappiness but, undoubtedly, the dominant feeling about Talbothays in the novel is of nature's abundance, and it is expressed most fully in the physical beauty of Tess herself. In this description she comes downstairs from her bed to start the afternoon skimming. She is observed by Angel Clare:

> *She had not heard him enter, and hardly realized his presence there. She was yawning, and he saw the red interior of her mouth as if it had been a snake's. She had stretched one arm so high above her coiled-up cable of hair that he could see its satin delicacy above the sunburn; her face was flushed with sleep, and her eyelids hung heavy over their pupils. The brim-fulness of her nature breathed from her. It was a moment when a woman's soul is more incarnate than at any other time; when the most spiritual beauty bespeaks itself flesh; and sex takes the outside place in the presentation.*[38]

At the opposite pole of the book is the exposed hill-top farm to the north of Dorchester called Flintcomb-Ash. Tess has been deserted by Angel, the seasonal work of Talbothays is ended, and she is forced to join the casual female labourers that Farmer Groby uses as his work force. The farm is vast and the work monotonous and dehumanizing. In the hundred-acre field where Tess and Marion grub for turnips, the brown face of the earth looks up at the white face of the sky *without anything standing between them but the two girls crawling over the surface of the field like flies. . . . Nobody came near them and their movements showed a mechanical regularity.*' When the frosts make work in the fields impossible, the work force is put to work drawing reeds in the barn. Here Tess finds Dark Car and the Queen of Diamonds,

> *those who had tried to fight with her in the midnight quarrel at Trantridge. They showed no recognition of her, and*

Contrast in *Tess*: '*The oozing fatness and warm ferments of the Froom Valley*'

Flintcomb-Ash, *'that starve-acre place'*

possibly had none, for they had been under the influence of liquor on that occasion, and were only temporary sojourners there as here. They did all kinds of men's work by preference, including well-sinking, hedging, ditching and excavating, without any sense of fatigue.[39]

In March, Izz and Tess are set to work on the threshing of the last rick of wheat. The threshing machine is described as *'the red tyrant that the women had come to serve'*, and Tess is given the job of feeding it. It is belt-driven from a steam engine which is worked by an engineer. Described as having the appearance of a creature from *'Tophet'*: *'He served fire and smoke.'* Touring Wessex with his steam engine, the Plutonic machine he serves, he has lost all contact with the land:

> *The long strap which ran from the driving-wheel of his engine to the red thresher under the rick was the sole tie-line between agriculture and him.*[40]

When the sun sets, Tess is seen in the red light, still mechanically working to the pace of the demonic machine. The suggestion of the assaults and tortures of hell is complete when the rats leave the rick. One of them leaps up the skirts of the half-tipsy Marion.

> *The rat was at last dislodged, . . . amid the barking of dogs, masculine shouts, feminine screams, oaths, stampings and confusion as of Pandemonium. . . .*[41]

At Flintcomb-Ash Tess experiences something akin to her rape at the hands of Alec d'Urberville. The red light and violence of the scene evoke memories of other moments in the book and anticipate the murder which is yet to come. But the section is also a magnificent evocation of the situation of itinerant farm labourers on the large, intensive, mechanized farms during the period of the 1870s in which the story is set.

The '*red tyrant*' in *Tess*: steam engine and threshing machine, around 1870 (by courtesy of Ransomes, Sims & Jefferies Ltd, Ipswich)

TIED COTTAGES, HIRING FAIRS AND LIVESTOCK FAIRS

'The Dorsetshire Labourer', the essay Hardy wrote for *Longman's Magazine* (July 1883), contains an attack on town-bred outsiders who think of the workfolk in terms of mumbling Hodge, the straw-in-hair yokel. He defends the subtlety of the Dorset dialect and commends the healthy outdoor life:

> . . . *a pure atmosphere and a pastoral environment are a very appreciable portion of the sustenance which tends to produce the sound mind and body.*

We are given a description of the hiring fairs at which the workfolk looking for employment declare their trade by their smocks and may be hired by a farmer who will seal the terms of the agreement with the exchange of a shilling. But changes have occurred:

> *the genuine white smock frock of Russia duck and the whitey-brown one of drabbet, are rarely seen now far afield, except on the shoulders of old men.*

Terms of employment are invariably reduced to writing.

Lady Day, the day on which, traditionally, the annual move of those changing jobs takes place, is described. The owner of the vacated tied cottage has about four hours between the departure of one family and the arrival of the next to whitewash it and clean it out. Hardy then tells a story to illustrate that only small beer was drunk on the day of the Lady Day removal. So far the tone of the essay has been light and evocatively descriptive; it now becomes harder and more factual as Hardy explains the changes in the nature of the agricultural work force and the effect that this is having on the local communities:

> *The annual migration from farm to farm is much in excess of what it was formerly. . . . They are also losing their peculiarities as a class . . . there are no nice homely workfolk now as there used to be. . . . The women have, in many districts, acquired the rollicking air of factory hands.—They are losing their individuality, but they are widening the range of their ideas and gaining in freedom. It is too much to expect them to remain stagnant and old-fashioned for the pleasure of spectators.*

Hardy has no doubt about the rights of workfolk to their freedom but he is anxious to record what is being lost:

> *Down to 20 or 30 years ago . . . the husbandman of either class had the interest of long personal association with his farm.*

Cottagers would plant their gardens, and improve the property when they were likely to stay there. They now had more money and freedom but *'they have lost touch with their environment'*. He notes the effect of migration of labourers on their children's education, in one instance thirty-five out of seventy-five scholars disappearing on one Lady Day. Flitting without paying rent owing was on the increase and it was little wonder that when lifehold leases expired, farmers were letting the tied cottages fall into disrepair. Most of these processes were long familiar by 1883.

We can see here many of the situations on which the plots of the novels turn. Perhaps the most recurrent theme is the collapse of the country community. Lady Day moves play key parts in *Far from the Madding Crowd*, *The Woodlanders* and in chapter fifty-one of *Tess of the d'Urbervilles*. In the latter two cases the emphasis is on the misfortune of the tenant whose life-lease is not renewed, but whereas Giles Winterborne is victimized, it seems entirely fair that the Durbeyfield family should be turned out.

Casterbridge Hiring Fair at which Gabriel Oak in *Far from the Madding Crowd* plays his flute and fails to get hired (chapter six) reappears in chapter twenty-three of *The Mayor of Casterbridge*.

The livestock fairs which appear in the novels also provide a barometer of agricultural change. Weydon Priors Fair (held at Weyhill, west of Andover in Hampshire, and famous largely for its sheep sales) appears twice in *The Mayor of Casterbridge*. By the time that Henchard and Susan appear, the business of the day is over. In the fair field they see

> *standing-places and pens where many hundreds of horses and sheep had been exhibited and sold in the forenoon.*

Among amusements offered are

> *peep-shows, toy-stands, waxworks, inspired monsters, disinterested medical men who travelled for the public good, thimble-riggers, nick-nack vendors, and readers of Fate.*[42]

It is at one such amusement tent that Troy in *Far from the Madding Crowd* turns up again after being believed drowned, using his equestrian skills to impersonate Dick Turpin in a spectacular dramatization. To this same fair, Greenhill Fair on Woodbury Hill, east of Bere Regis, Joseph Poorgrass is taken to cure his bashfulness looking at the '*women riding round — standing upon horses, with hardly anything on but their smocks*'. And, typical of the bogus medical tricksters is Vilbert in *Jude the Obscure* who uses Jude to obtain orders for '*Physician Vilbert's golden ointment, life-drops and female pills*'. He later reappears at the great Agricultural Show at Stoke Barehills (Basingstoke in Hampshire) where Arabella buys a love philtre from him.

On going to Weydon Priors on the first occasion Henchard had been told of the pulling down of cottages in the area and when, some eighteen years later, Susan returns, she notices various mechanical improvements in the roundabouts:

> *But the real business of the fair had considerably dwindled. The new periodical great markets of neighbouring towns were beginning to interfere seriously with the trade carried on here for centuries.*[43]

The coming of the railway to the south-west and the new significance of machinery had caused this decline by the late 1840s. At the end of the book Henchard reaches Weydon Priors on his sixth day away from Casterbridge:

> *The renowned hill whereupon the annual fair had been held for generations was now bare of human beings, and almost of ought beside.*[44]

SEASONAL CUSTOMS

Among Hardy's manuscripts can be found many instances of his wish to preserve parts of the village culture that was disappearing so fast: country dances, songs, customs and local stories.

His text of the Christmas mummers' play, *St George and the Turkish Knight*, is as useful to the folklorist as its performance was to Eustacia as a means of glimpsing Clym (*The Return of the Native*). The play enacts a fight, a death and a return to life and ends with a celebration. Traditionally these mummers' plays were held at the turning point of the year and are in origin pagan enactments of the death of the old year and rebirth of the new. The same person or member of his family would play the same part each year and his costume would be kept, repaired and elaborated by the family from year to year. Local variants in character, script and costume are common.

We have several instances of village club-walking. In *Under the Greenwood Tree* Reuben Dewey is married on White Tuesday, the day of the Mellstock club-walking, and after the wedding they march '*two and two around the parish*'. In *Tess of the d'Urbervilles* Angel Clare first sees Tess at the Marlott May Day club-walking:

> *It had walked for hundred of years, if not as a benefit club, as a votive sisterhood of some sort ; . . . Its singularity lay less in the retention of . . . walking in procession and dancing on each anniversary than in the members being solely women.*[45]

The Midsummer Eve customs have a central part in *The Woodlanders* when Fitzpiers pursues the girls as they scatter from their meeting in the woods on the stroke of midnight. Mrs Penny in *Under the Greenwood Tree* exclaims as she flops into a chair:

> '. . . *my heart hasn't been in such a thumping state since I used to sit up on Old Midsummer Eve to see who my husband was going to be.*'

The Return of the Native leans heavily on such seasonal devices for its shape. The autumnal bonfire (traditionally held on 5 November commemorating Guy Fawkes but, of course, pagan in origin) on Rainbarrow sets the scene against which we see Eustacia, and it burns as a metaphor throughout the book. After her marriage she meets Damon Wildeve at a gypsying which is clearly a Midsummer bonfire:

> *For the time Paganism was revived in their hearts, the pride of life was all in all, and they adored none other than themselves.*[46]

Seasonal customs and primitive notions relating to devils and witchcraft are rife on Egdon Heath. The Maypole dance outside Thomasin's house on the edge of the heath is rather in contrast in feeling but still basically instinctual and pagan:

> *The instincts of merry England lingered on here with exceptional vitality, and the symbolic customs which*

tradition has attached to each season of the year were yet a reality on Egdon. Indeed, the impulses of all such outlandish hamlets are pagan still . . .[47]

THE DEMON DRINK

The dangers of drink are amply illustrated in the pages of Hardy's novels. Henchard gets drunk on furmity laced with rum at Weydon Priors Fair and sells his wife. Troy forces brandy and hot water on his labouring force at the harvest supper and dance thus rendering them incapable, and placing the harvest at risk from the storm. And if Jan Coggan, he of the multiplying eye, had not stopped to strengthen his courage with ale at the Bucks Head, Troytown, the mortal remains of Fanny Robin and her child would have reached their resting place that day and Bathsheba Everdene would not have seen them. The time that the parents of Tess Durbeyfield spend at Rollivers is a major cause of their inadequacy as parents and there are many such moments in the novels when the puritanically minded could point a neat moral. But we should not stop there.

Hardy's tone when he talks of drink is usually one of affection as when, in the 1895 Preface to *Far from the Madding Crowd*, he laments *'the love of fuddling'* as one of the old ways that have disappeared from the village of Weatherbury. Drink played a major part in the working and social lives of Dorset workfolk and, as we should expect, this fact is reflected in Hardy's portrayal of them. The staple drink of the Dorset labourer was either cider or beer. Field workers often carried small pot containers called cider owls strapped to their belts. Henchard, though teetotal himself, brews beer for his workfolk and the best beer in Dorchester, landlord Stannidge's twelve-bushel ale, is said to be *'the chief attraction'* of The Three Mariners. The band and choir of All Saints Church (*The Mayor of Casterbridge*) go in there after church on Sunday to discuss the sermon and drink a regulation half-pint out of cups

> *straight-sided with two leafless lime trees done in eel brown on the sides, one towards the drinker's lips, the other towards his comrade.*[48]

It was in the same pub that Michael Mail in *Under the Greenwood Tree* recalled sitting, eating and chewing in time to the music when a brass band struck up outside.[49] Harmony, a dominant theme in that novel, verges on the farcical here, but the story is told at the tranter's party where several generations of neighbours meet to celebrate Christmas.

At Warren's Malthouse (*Far from the Madding Crowd*) the aged maltster drinks cider with his son and grandson using the old loving cup which would be passed from hand to hand:

> *Jacob stooped to the God-forgive-me, which was a two-handled tall mug standing in the ashes, cracked and charred with heat: it was rather furred with extraneous matter about the outside, especially in the crevices of the handles, the innermost curves of which may not have seen daylight for several years by reason of this encrustation thereon— formed of ashes accidentally wetted with cider and baked hard ; but to the mind of any sensible drinker the cup was no worse for that, being incontestably clean on the inside and about the rim. It may be observed that such a class of mug is called a God-forgive-me in Weatherbury and its vicinity for uncertain reasons; probably because its size makes any given toper feel ashamed of himself when he sees its bottom in drinking it empty.*[50]

The cup itself is one instance of the bonds of community between the men and of the continuation of the past into the present that we associate with the rustics.

To Mark Clark cider is his '*only doctor*', and I think that most readers will agree with Joseph Poorgrass when he anticipates the shearing feast with the words:

> '*Yes; victuals and drink is a cheerful thing, and gives nerves to the nerveless, if the form of words may be used. 'Tis the gospel of the body, without which we perish, so to speak.*'[51]

However, we have a more ambiguous reaction to a similar sentiment expressed in the Buck's Head when Coggan asserts:

> '*Too much liquor is bad, and leads us to that horned man in the smoky house ; but after all, many people haven't the gift of enjoying a wet, and since we be highly favoured with a power that way, we should make the most o't.*'
> '*True,*' said Mark Clark. ''*Tis a talent the lord has mercifully bestowed upon us, and we ought not to neglect it . . .*'[52]

Drink in Hardy: The King's Arms, Dorchester

We remember the result of this drinking session and note that Gabriel Oak, the hero of the novel, who enters in a moment, is a temperate man.

In *The Woodlanders* drink is a natural part of the working scene. Melbury and Winterborne discuss Grace's plight over a cup of ale mulled in the ashes, and of the drink at Winterborne's party Robert Creedle comments:

> '*Good honest drink 'twere, the headiest drink I ever brewed; and the best wine that berries could rise to; and the briskest Horner-and-Cleeves cider ever wrung down, leaving out the spice and sperrits I put into it, while that egg-flip would ha' passed through muslin, so little criddled 'twere.*'[53]

At the timber auction there is

> *a barrel of strong ale for the select, and cider in milking-pails into which anybody dipped who chose.*[54]

The brew house on a farm in which beer or cider was made for the workfolk became the social centre, for obvious reasons. In such circumstances, the quality of the local brew would become a point of pride. The Little Hintock cider-house keeper, Mr Cawtree, scorns Shottsford:

> '. . . *you can't victual your carcase there unless you've got money; and you can't buy a cup of genuine there, whether or no* . . .'[55]

What is attractive about the cider houses and local inns that we meet in the novels is the opportunity they provide for people to meet, talk, reminisce and reassert their links with one another. But in the later novels, *Tess of the d'Urbervilles* and *Jude the Obscure*, the pub is becoming something rather different. The girls on d'Urberville's farm go to Chaseborough simply to get drunk, and the beer they drink is no longer brewed locally. They

Cider drinkers on a farm (University of Reading, Museum of English Rural Life)

spend Sunday

> *in sleeping off the dyspeptic effects of the curious compounds*
> *sold them as beer by the monopolizers of the once*
> *independent inns.*[56]

The tragedy lies not only in the production of liquor which
Spinks[57] might have called *'a disgrace to the name of stimmilent'*
but in the death of the local pub as a centre of a working
community.

Before the seventeenth century, when West Indian sugar
became available in England, mead was a common drink. By the
nineteenth century it had been superseded by beer and cider in
the towns but was still brewed in country areas. Mrs Crick, in
Tess, sends a bottle of mead to Angel Clare's mother as a gift.
Geoffrey Day, Lord Wessex's keeper (*Under the Greenwood
Tree*) is taking a swarm of bees when Dick Dewey visits him, as
is Bathsheba (*Far from the Madding Crowd*) when Troy comes to
invite her to see his sword-drill. The two drinks made from the
honey, mead and metheglin (a word derived from the Welsh for
healing liquor), are distinguished in the short story from *Wessex
Tales* called 'The Three Strangers'. Shepherd Fennel's wife
serves her guests with strong mead *'brewed of the purest first-year
or maiden honey, four pounds to the gallon—with its due complement
of white of eggs, cinnamon, ginger, cloves, mace, rosemary, yeast and
processes of working, bottling, and cellaring'* and it is strong enough
to make a hangman sing! In fact this brew sounds more like
metheglin, which differs from mead in being spiced. The
strength of Keeper Day's metheglin is referred to more than once
in the novels. After drinking it and hearing an owl go 'Whoo' in
the woods, Joseph Poorgrass replied *'Joseph Poorgrass of
Weatherbury'*. This shy man is given the strength to tell the story
by the mulled cider in Warren's Malthouse.[58] The hospitable
William Dewey, expert on music and cider alike, provides the
Mellstock choir with similar stimulus when they meet to practise
in his cottage.[59]

Hardy himself drank very little alcohol but, even as an old
man, he delighted in visiting the old Dorset inns, so many of
which appear in his stories. For an inn is to a village what a
kitchen is to a house, the place where people meet, talk and eat
and drink together, and it is there that you will learn most about
them.

DIALECT

In a review in September 1872 Hardy's friend, Horace Moule, noted *'an occasional tendency of the country folk . . . to express themselves in the language of the author's manner of thought, rather than their own'*. Hardy, on the other hand, expresses his intention thus:

> *. . . to show mainly the character of the speakers and only to give a general idea of their linguistic peculiarities.*[60]

An exact phonetic representation of dialect speech would be very difficult to follow, but the compromise that Hardy puts into the mouths of his rustics is no crude approximation. He goes far beyond the easy literary devices of making rustics drop their 'g's and 'h's, say ''em' for 'them', 'was' for 'were', and spice their utterances with gnomic proverbs. In a letter to the *Spectator*[61] he claimed that his method was that of *'scrupulously preserving the local idiom, together with the words which have no synonyms among those in general use'*. We may categorize these dialect forms simply.

Easily worked out are dialect pronunciations of familiar words: *feymel*–female; *martel*–mortal; *ghastly*–ghostly; *arrant*–errand; *trate*–treat; *clane*–clean; *kep*–keep; *criddled*–curdled; *chield*–child; *zid*–saw; *ballet*–ballad. The Dorset accent also inserts a 'w' which will be familiar to the readers of T. F. Powys or William Barnes: *cwome*–come; *hwome*–home; *wold*–old; *cwomely*–comely; and even *cwoffer*–coffer.

Many modern readers will require a glossary to explain various words connected with agriculture, flowers, food or garments as well as for local games and traditions. Dialect words are also used to describe rural trades. Those in the novels who work on dairy farms talk of *nott cows*, *rawmil cheese* and cows that have *gone azew;* workfolk in general use words such as *linhay, mixen, speaker* and *stitches;* those especially concerned with thatching are familiar with *reeds* and *ricking rods;* cider-making has its own vocabulary (*cheese, pummy, wring-down* and words denoting various kinds of apple) and this is also the case with copse-work (*gad, rendle-wood, shrouding*).

Among words probably used because of their expressiveness can be mentioned many words of abuse such as *gawk-hammer, sappy* and *stunpoll*, and adjectives denoting negative qualities e.g., *draw-latching, lammocken, scammish, thirtingill, teuny, mandy, mafrotite* and *slack-twisted*.

A group of dialect inversions is easy enough to grasp: *here-right* for right here; *home-along* for along home, and *near-foot-afore* for near fore-foot.

But I think that among the most attractive, though few have survived outside the novels, are some of the older dialect words. Usually in their context it is easy to guess their meaning: *dumbledores*–bumblebees; *dazed*–astonished; *efts*–newts; *ents*–ants; *fuddle*–booze-up; *fay*–proper; *fall*–veil or autumn; *glutch*–swallow; *hontish*–proud; *I'll be jowned if I do*–I'll be damned if I do; *keacorn*–windpipe; *larry* or *nunnywatch*–a disturbance; and *wambling*–walking unsteadily or, elsewhere, with a wiggle.

Put in a list like that they lose their strength and particularly the rhythms and emphasis they had originally, whether in Warren's Malthouse or Tranter Dewey's cottage. That the rustics sound right is probably the best test of the authenticity of the dialect. In a letter to the *Pall Mall Gazette* Hardy indicated its importance in the novels:

> *All that I know about the Dorset labourers I gathered . . . from living in the country as a child and from thoroughly knowing their dialect. You cannot get at the labourer otherwise. Dialect is the only pass-key to anything like intimacy.*[62]

Recent studies of nineteenth-century dialect forms in Dorset show the remarkable strength and accuracy of Hardy's literary approximation.[63]

FOLKLORE: WEATHER LORE AND FOLK CURES

We are told in Steinmetz's *A Manual of Weathercasts* (1886), a book Hardy owned and consulted closely, that most of the natural phenomena that indicate weather change have scientific explanations. For example, as it becomes more humid a spider's web will become more heavy, and so spiders dropping to the ground are noted as a sign of approaching rain. Countrymen see such signs and know what they mean. When Gabriel Oak saw a toad crossing the road, '*he knew what this message from the Great Mother meant*'. Other indications that there is to be a great storm at Weatherbury[64] are that garden slugs come indoors, spiders drop from the roof, and sheep huddle in the corner of a field, their backs facing the approaching storm.

When the Egdon Conjuror, Mr Fall, predicts the harvest weather for the Mayor of Casterbridge, his method depends largely on the interpretation of natural phenomena:

> '*By the sun, moon, and stars, by the clouds, the winds, the trees and grass, the candle flame and swallows, the smell of the herbs; likewise by the cats' eyes, the ravens, the leeches, the spiders, and the dung-mixen, the last fortnight in August will be—rain and tempest.*'[65]

One does not feel entirely comfortable about the cats' eyes, but the rest could simply be natural intimations of weather change, a more complex equivalent of the common-sense observation of Marty South in *The Woodlanders* when she sees three pheasants roosting at the end of a bough:

> '*If it were going to be stormy they'd squeeze close to the trunk.*'[66]

Another of Conjuror Fall's skills was the curing of warts by a method not unlike shock therapy, the toad bag. The shock said to effect the cure was brought about by the movement of a toad inside a bag tied to the affected place. For more serious cases, such as wems or goitres, a more violent '*turning of the blood*' was required and this could be done by applying the affected area to the broken neck of a newly hanged man. Conjuror Trendle recommends this expedient to cure Gertrude Lodge's withered arm in one of Hardy's best short stories, 'The Withered Arm'.

The traditional association of love with turtle doves doubtless lies behind Vilbert's love potion made from pigeons' hearts (*Jude the Obscure*); but the idea of like curing like accounts for the traditional cure for adder-bite used in *The Return of the Native*:

> '*You must rub the place with the fat of other adders and the only way to get that is by frying them.*'[67]

It will not surprise the student of folklore to learn that recently it has been found that there is a sound medical benefit from this treatment.

SUPERSTITIONS, OMENS AND PREDICTIONS

It is sometimes difficult to see whether Hardy is drawing on widely known folklore or simply creating a natural symbol. In

The Woodlanders[68] for example, two large birds quarrel and tumble into the wood fire, and this foreshadows the later problems of Grace and Fitzpiers. Closer to folklore is the use of the literary symbol of the nightingale found at the end of *Under the Greenwood Tree* (it was said in Greek legend that Philomel was raped by King Tereus and then changed into a nightingale to prevent her telling of it). The cuckoo, a bird that has long symbolized infidelity in love, makes pointed appearances both in *The Woodlanders*[69] and *Far from the Madding Crowd*[70].

Good luck is attributed to Christian Cantle because he is born with a caul on his head (*The Return of the Native*) and when Dick Dewey's bees swarm on his wedding day this is seen as an excellent omen (*Under the Greenwood Tree*). More frequent in the novels are bad omens: the crowing of a cock three times on the day of Tess's wedding[71] or the breaking of a key.[72] A bad dream can bode ill-fortune—Joseph Poorgrass has one on the night Fanny Robin disappears:

> *'What a night of horrors!' murmured Joseph Poorgrass, waving his hands spasmodically. 'I've had the news-bell ringing in my left ear bad enough for a murder, and I've seen a magpie all alone!'*[73]

Grace Melbury's ominous dream of crazed marriage bells on the eve of her marriage is confirmed in the ill-luck of her match with Fitzpiers. Christian Cantle's fear that it was an evil omen to dream of one's shadow in the shape of a coffin (*The Return of the Native*) was derived from a story told to Hardy by his servant, Anne, while they lived at Sturminster.

Curses on whole families are found in *Tess of the d'Urbervilles* and in *Jude the Obscure*. A death in the d'Urberville family is foreshadowed by the appearance of the d'Urberville coach.

When Tess pricks her chin on a rose thorn she sees this as an ill omen:

> *Like all the cottagers in Blackmoor Vale, Tess was steeped in fancies and prefigurative superstitions; she thought this an ill omen—the first she had noted that day.*[74]

Another instance of local superstition is the belief at Talbothays that the butter will not form in the churn because one of the milkmaids is in love.[75]

In Hardy's *Life* he tells a curious tale of his dog, Wessex. On the evening of 18 April 1925, he was visited at Max Gate by the

Secretary of The Society of Dorset Men in London. Wessex leapt up to greet the visitor but then suddenly retreated and started to whine and would not go near him. The next day Hardy learnt that this gentleman who had left Max Gate at about 10 pm had died about an hour after returning to his hotel in Dorchester.

The true is often as inexplicable as the fictional, and Hardy never conveys in the novels that he views superstition as a sign of ignorance. Eustacia Vye takes this view of the people of Egdon but it is not the view of the author. At the age of 74 he wrote:

> *I "believe" (in the modern sense of the word) not only in the things Bergson believes in, but in spectres, mysterious voices, intuitions, omens, dreams, haunted places etc. etc.*[76]

DIVINATION AND WITCHCRAFT

The belief that certain gifted individuals have special powers to see into the future and effect cures still persists, and not only in country areas. It is very much in evidence in the mid-nineteenth-century setting of Hardy's novels.

Henchard consults Conjuror Fall to ascertain the weather. Conjuror Mynterne, an historical figure, is referred to in Hardy's *Life*[77] as having predicted the death of the husband of Patt Pimm. A local legend at Batcombe Downe (near Cerne Abbas) suggests that part of an old tomb that used to touch the outer wall of the Minterne aisle in Batcombe Church covers the grave of *'Conjuring Minterne'*, who vowed that he would be buried neither in the church nor out of it.

Hardy's fictional conjuror, Conjuror Trendle of Egdon, discovers the identity of the woman who has overlooked Gertrude Lodge's withered arm by looking into egg-white suspended in water ('The Withered Arm'). Rhoda in the same story, like Elizabeth Endorfield in *Under the Greenwood Tree*, has gained the local reputation of being a witch. Eustacia Vye, *'the lonesome dark-eyed creature up there that some say is a witch'* as she is described by Timothy Fairways,[78] has a long stocking-needle stuck into her one day in church by Susan Nunsuch who believes that Eustacia is *'overlooking'* her children. Ironically, Eustacia dies shortly after Susan Nunsuch had made a wax effigy of her, stuck it with pins and melted it while reciting the Lord's Prayer backwards three times.[79]

George Pickingill (born 1816), a conjuror from Canewdon

We are told of Henchard in *The Mayor of Casterbridge* that '*the sense of the supernatural was strong in this unhappy man*'.[80] When his fortunes are at their lowest he comments:

> '*I wonder if it can be that somebody has been roasting a waxen image of me, or stirring an unholy brew to confound me!*'[81]

A similar fear of the supernatural is shown by Melbury's ostler who believes that Grace's mare has been '*hag-rid*', that is, ridden by witches during the night; and earlier in the same novel, at the bark-stripping in the forest, his men tell stories of white and black witches and '*the spirits of the two brothers*'.[82]

Various magical rites were traditionally conducted on Midsummer Eve in connection with love and marriage. Jude, after Sue has returned to Phillotson, sits alone on Midsummer Eve,

Mother Louse, the traditional conception of a witch (Mary Evans Picture Library)

"Linda Maestra" by Francisco Goya, showing a young witch being instructed by an experienced hag (The Fotomas Index)

Popular images of witches: woodcuts, probably dating from the early nineteenth century (Bodleian Library, Oxford)

hoping to see the phantom of his beloved wife[83]: we may compare this with the poem 'On A Midsummer Eve'. A more complex spell to see who her husband would be was tried by Mrs Penny in *Under the Greenwood Tree*, with more success:

> '*I put the bread-and-cheese and beer quite ready, as the witch's book ordered, and I opened the door and I waited till the clock struck twelve . . . and when the clock had struck, lo and behold I could see through the door a little small man in the lane wi a shoemaker's apron.*[84]

Other Midsummer Eve spells are referred to in *The Woodlanders*, such as digging a hole at midnight and listening to hear your husband's trade, and sowing hempseed; and the pagan Midsummer Eve ceremony is still enacted in the wood at midnight by the local village girls. It is done half out of tradition, half in jest, but, appropriately, Grace runs into the arms of her future husband, Dr Fitzpiers.

Bathsheba Everdene in *Far from the Madding Crowd* is again half in jest when she uses the ancient method of divination of placing a key in a family Bible opposite a specified verse in the Book of Ruth in order to see if someone loves her:

> *The verse was repeated; the book turned round; Bathsheba blushed guiltily.*[85]

A final instance of witchcraft is taken not from any novel but from Hardy's *Life*. It illustrates both Hardy's interest in the occult as well as the widespread nature of these beliefs:

> *Among the many stories of spell-working that I have been told is one of how it was done by two girls in 1830. They killed a pigeon, stuck its heart full of pins, made a tripod of three knitting needles, and suspended the heart on them over a lamp, murmuring an incantation while it roasted, and using the name of the young man in whom one or both were interested. The said young man felt racking pains about the region of the heart, and suspecting something went to the constables. The girls were sent to prison.*[86]

EDUCATION

In the cultured and affluent London society in which Hardy mixed for most of his working life, an educated man would be understood to have gone to a public school and either Oxford or Cambridge. Hardy's very different path, having left Last's Academy at the age of sixteen, is reflected not only in certain unfortunate stylistic faults, for example an eagerness to parade erudition in learned allusions, but also in his interest in education as a theme in his novels. Driven by his mother's fears and ambitions Hardy attained a high degree of education in his youth, and the habits of hard work and persistent acquisition of new knowledge learnt then never left him. On the other hand, he had grown away from the country people and the village life that his father valued so highly. It is hardly surprising that we find education in the novels appearing both as a means of social advancement (Gabriel Oak and Jude are two obvious self-taught heroes) and, somewhat in contradiction, as one of the forces that has divorced man from his village community and the intuitive knowledge gained from a life working on the land.

Fancy Day, the new Mellstock schoolmistress in *Under the Greenwood Tree*, has been educated away from simple acceptance of Dick Dewey as her lover. She has learnt caprice and widened her scope in the search for a partner to encompass Shiner and Parson Maybold. One senses at the end that the simple Dick Dewey will not find her an easy partner. Grace Melbury is another girl educated out of her social milieu. Her father, having been taunted for his poor learning as a boy, has given his daughter a schooling that costs him nearly £100 a year. When she returns to Little Hintock she has forgotten the difference between bitter-sweets and John-apple trees, is embarrassed by Winterborne's country ways and falls for the shallow sophistication of Mrs Charmond and Dr Fitzpiers. But when Giles dies she recognizes '*how little acquirements and culture weigh beside sterling personal character*'.[87]

However, for most of Hardy's heroes and heroines education is desirable, as in the case of Elizabeth-Jane in *The Mayor of Casterbridge*. Tess in *Tess of the d'Urbervilles* has acquired an education above that of the majority of Marnhull girls or Talbothays milkmaids. She

> *had passed the Sixth Standard in the National School under a London-trained mistress, spoke two languages; the dialect at home, more or less; ordinary English abroad and to persons of quality.*[88]

Yet in the same book there is considerable scorn for Angel

Clare's two brothers who are described as *'such unimpeachable models as are turned out yearly by the lathe of a systematic tuition'.*[89] They have schooling but very little feeling.

Like Tess, Gabriel Oak has learnt much. from living and working in the country. He tells the time from the stars and can read nature's warnings of the approaching storm. But he is also a man who has acquired skills from books. Those he takes with him from his shepherd's hut indicate the areas of his study: *The Young Man's Best Companion, The Farrier's Sure Guide, The Veterinary Surgeon, Paradise Lost, The Pilgrim's Progress, Robinson Crusoe,* Ash's *Dictionary* and Wallingame's *Arithmetic.*[90] He also plays the flute and has professional skills both as shepherd and bailiff. This is no simple son of the soil but a capable and ambitious man who sees education, as Hardy did, as a means to self-improvement.

The emphasis in *Jude the Obscure* has changed. An attack on social injustice in the field of education is a major theme, though perhaps secondary to that of the psychology of Sue and Jude. Jude, like Oak, is a self-taught man, but whereas Oak was thwarted only by Fate (in losing his sheep) and Bathsheba, Jude is thwarted by Fate, by his own emotional nature, by Sue and by the social injustice of the entry system of the University of Christminster. Unlike Oak, Jude has lost any intimacy with nature, and in this he is a modern. Yet in him can still be seen the two strangely differing attitudes to education we have found in the novels: education as a means of betterment, and education as a source of discontent and personal bewilderment.

[1] Thomas Hardy *Far from the Madding Crowd* Chap. 22   [2] *ibid*. Chap. 4   [3] Thomas Hardy *The Woodlanders* Chap. 8 p. 103   [4]*ibid*. Chap. 44 p. 428   [5] *ibid*. Chap. 4 p. 56   [6] *ibid*. Chap. 3 p. 46   [7] *ibid*. Chap. 4 p. 55   [8] *ibid*. Chap. 4 p. 57   [9] *ibid*. Chap. 28 pp. 275–276   [10] *ibid*. Chap. 48 p. 473   [11] *ibid*. Chap. 1 p. 31   [12] *ibid*. Chap. 3 p. 45   [13] *ibid*. Chap. 4 p. 54   [14] *ibid*. Chap. 8 p. 104   [15] *ibid*. Chap. 7 pp. 89–90   [16] *ibid*. Chap. 42 p. 405   [17] Thomas Hardy *The Mayor of Casterbridge* Chap. 4 pp. 63–64   [18] *ibid*. Chap. 22 p. 211   [19] *ibid*. Chap. 9 p. 101   [20] *ibid*. Chap. 9 p. 103   [21] *ibid*. Chap. 27 p. 257   [22] *ibid*. Chap. 23 p. 220   [23] *ibid*. Chap. 36 p. 327   [24] *ibid*. Chap. 32 pp. 291–292   [25] *ibid*. Chap. 26 pp. 245–246   [26] *ibid*. Chap. 14 p. 138 and Chap. 19 p. 179   [27] *ibid*. Chap. 8 pp. 91–92   [28] *ibid*. Chap. 21 p. 196   [29] *ibid*. Chap. 27 p. 253   [30] *ibid*. Chap. 11 p. 113   [31] *ibid*. Chap. 11 p. 114   [32] *ibid*. Chap. 19 p. 178   [33] Thomas Hardy *Tess of the d'Urbervilles* Chap. 5 p. 78   [34] *ibid*. Chap. 17 p. 183   [35] *ibid*. Chap. 19 p. 195   [36] *ibid*. Chap. 19 p. 195   [37] *ibid*. Chap. 24 p. 227   [38] *ibid*. Chap. 27 p. 254   [39] *ibid*. Chap. 43 p. 405   [40] *ibid*. Chap. 47 p. 450   [41] *ibid*. Chap. 48 p. 462   [42] as 17, Chap. 1 p. 37   [43] *ibid*. Chap. 3 p. 53   [44] *ibid*. Chap. 44 p. 401   [45] as 33, Chap. 2 p. 47   [46] Thomas Hardy *The Return of the Native* Bk. 4 Chap. 3 p. 342   [47] *ibid*. Bk. 6 Chap. 1 p. 489   [48] as 17, Chap. 33 p. 300   [49] Thomas Hardy *Under the Greenwood Tree* Chap. 8 p. 91   [50] as 1, Chap. 8 p. 96   [51] *ibid*. Chap. 22 p. 209   [52] *ibid*. Chap. 42 p. 364   [53] as 3, Chap. 10 p. 122   [54] *ibid*. Chap. 7 p. 91   [55] *ibid*. Chap. 4 p. 62   [56] as 33, Chap. 10 p. 112   [57] as 49, p. 43   [58] as 1, Chap. 8 p. 100   [59] as 49, Chap. 3   [60] *Athenaeum*, 30 November 1878   [61] *Spectator*, 15 October 1881   [62] letter to the *Pall Mall Gazette*, 2 January 1892   [63] *Studies in English Dialect* (1967–1968) (The Institute of Dialect and Folk Life Studies, University of Leeds); Ulla Baugner 'A Study of the use of Dialect in Thomas Hardy's Novels and Short Stories with Special Reference to Phonology and Vocabulary' (Stockholm Theses 7, 1972); F. B. Pinion *A Hardy Companion* (Macmillan, 1968) for a general glossary   [64] as 1, Chap. 36 pp. 312ff.   [65] as 17, Chap. 26 p. 245   [66] as 3, Chap. 9 p. 110   [67] as 46, Bk. 4 Chap. 7 p. 383   [68] as 3, Chap. 19 p. 198   [69] *ibid*. Chap. 37 p. 359   [70] as 1, Chap. 19 p. 177   [71] as 33, Chap. 33 p. 311   [72] as 1, Chap. 33, p. 287   [73] *ibid*. Chap. 6 p. 87   [74] as 33, Chap. 6 p. 208   [76] *Life* p. 370   [77] *ibid*. 4 December 1884   [78] as 46, Bk. 1 Chap. 5 p. 96   [79] *ibid*. Bk. 5 Chap. 7 p. 456   [80] as 17, Chap. 41 p. 376   [81] *ibid*. Chap. 27 p. 253   [82] as 3, Chap. 28 p. 271 and Chap. 19 p. 193   [83] Thomas Hardy *Jude the Obscure* Bk. 3 Chap. 8   [84] as 49, Chap. 8 p. 88   [85] as 1, Chap. 13 p. 143   [86] as 76   [87] as 3, Chap. 45 p. 433   [88] as 33, Chap. 3 p. 58   [89] *ibid*. Chap. 25 p. 241   [90] as 1, Chap. 8 p. 113

4

Hardy's Distinctive Views

1. THE WAGGERY OF FATE

This phrase comes from Hardy's description of Clym Yeobright's career from heath-boy to Paris jeweller and then back to turf-cutter (*The Return of the Native*). We often find Fate portrayed as a joker playing cruel jests on mankind. At the end of *Tess of the d'Urbervilles* when Tess dies on the scaffold at Wintonchester, Hardy writes that the President of the Immortals '*had ended his sport with Tess*'.[1] The Gods are invariably malicious in Hardy, perpetrating tragedies which have no comprehensible meaning. In *The Mayor of Casterbridge* he writes of '*the ingenious machinery contrived by the Gods for reducing human possibilities of amelioration to a minimum*'[2] and he describes Marty and Winterborne in *The Woodlanders* thus:

> *And yet their lonely courses formed no detached design at all, but were part of the pattern in the great web of human doings then weaving in both hemispheres from the White Sea to Cape Horn.*[3]

In this last statement we see that Hardy has not abandoned the idea of God; there are still forces working on man's destiny even if they do ignore the isolated individual. These forces are personified in his play *The Dynasts*, written after he had stopped writing novels.

In a poem about the sinking of the Titanic (on 15 April 1912), our attention is drawn to the coming together of the iceberg and the ship. The force that brings them together Hardy calls '*the Immanent Will that stirs and urges everything*':

ix
Alien they seemed to be:
No mortal eye could see
The intimate wedding of their later history,

x
Or sign that they were bent
By paths coincident
On being anon twin halves of one august event,

xi
Till the Spinner of the Years
Said 'Now!' And each one hears
And consummation comes, and jars two hemispheres.[4]

The idea of the '*Immanent Will*' does suggest that there is a global destiny being worked out, a web that has not yet been spun. It is given a different emphasis in a passage from *The Woodlanders* where it appears as the '*Unfulfilled Intention*'.[5] Though the means by which it works seem to be cruel and sinister, the Intention is nevertheless there. A phrase in *Tess*

The real world as symbol: '*The leaf was crippled, the taper was interrupted: the lichen ate the stalk, and the ivy strangled to death the promising sapling.*' (*The Woodlanders* Chap. 7 p. 90)

acknowledges a similar power at work but suggests not so much an intention that has not yet been worked out as a good plan that went wrong in the working, '*the ill-judged execution of the well-judged plan of things*'.[6] Notably in the novels this power thwarts love, causes cruel coincidence or unhappy chance and is expressed in nature as much as in human affairs. More of a feeling about life than a systematic philosophical position, it is perhaps best expressed in a note he wrote as a young man of thirty, accepting '*Mother's notion (and also mine)—that a figure stands in our van with arms uplifted, to knock us back from any pleasant prospect we indulge in as probable*'.

However, whenever we meet an instance of this idea in the novels it is as well to examine carefully the context in which it appears. Especially in the earlier novels there is invariably some balancing human being who supplies the love and attention that the Gods will not supply. It is too simple to describe Hardy as a pessimist.

2. RELIGION

Hardy says one thing in his *Life* about religion, and another in his novels. In the novels there is satire of the Church, there are attacks on outmoded doctrine and there is constant questioning of the existence of a loving God, but at no point in the novels does Hardy, as author, deny the existence of God. That Hardy in fact lost his faith some time during the 1860s as a result of studying various contemporary writers recommended to him by Horace Moule is reflected in the novels, but the author's tone in them is not that of the dogmatic atheist but rather that of the sceptical rationalist, drawing attention to the sadder facts of human existence and frankly disbelieving that any loving God could have planned things that way.

In the middle years of the nineteenth century some very old assumptions about God and the Bible were being questioned. This process had started well before Darwin, in his *Origin of Species*, suggested the evolutionary theory of natural selection and that man was descended from the lower primates. Sir Charles Lyell's *The Principles of Geology* (1830–33) taught that the whole of the earth's surface was, and always had been, in a state of slow change. These findings questioned outright the claim of the Bible that God created the Universe and man in six days.

Darwin's *Origin of Species*
(1859) mocked in a cartoon
(Radio Times Hulton Picture
Library)

A group of German philosophers and Biblical scholars known as
the Christologists had also attacked the authority of the Bible.
Reimarus (1694–1768) interpreted the whole Bible from
Abraham to St Paul as a specimen of human depravity and error.
Schleiermacher (1768–1834) explained Jesus as only superhumanly
good, not divine, and threw doubt on the authenticity of all the
gospels except St John's. Another influential writer, Strauss
(1808–74), who entered the ministry but then turned apostate,
criticized the historical accuracy of the New Testament: it was, he
claimed, a mere Jewish dream of a national hero and certainly not
the authentic word of God.

Scholars in England had similar doubts. A book published in 1860 called *Essays and Reviews* contained pieces by seven eminent contributors, nicknamed 'The Seven against Christ', who reverently but critically attempted to expose the inaccuracies, anachronisms and errors of fact in the first six books of the Bible.

If the voice of God was not to be found in the Bible, neither was the hand of God to be found in society. Mill's *Principles of Political Economy* (1848) showed that society is swayed by economic factors. Malthus (1766–1834), whose studies of population growth provided the rationale for birth control, gave a picture of humanity that was a human equivalent of Darwin's '*survival of the fittest*'. The poor, he argued, will always multiply and compete against each other for employment. Carried to its extremest expression, the idea is found in Harriet Martineau's *Letters On The Laws of Man's Social Nature and Development* (1851), where she argues that the area of man's control over his life is limited to his own body and that God's control over either man or society appears to be negligible.

To many people now, these issues may not seem particularly important, but at the time Hardy was beginning to write they were of vital importance to him and to many of his readers. Brought up on the Bible and regular Anglican church-going, as an adult he was faced with scientific, Biblical, economic and sociological scholarship that questioned the medieval idea of God. There was also something in his own temperament that favoured the idea that life is essentially tragic and misdirected.

At his mildest in the novels Hardy simply mocks vanity in churchmen: for example, that of the Bath clergymen with their fine ornaments whom Cainy Ball has seen in *Far from the Madding Crowd*. In contrast is the local, kindly Parson Thirdly who gives Poorgrass his seed potatoes when all those of Poorgrass have been frosted. In this same book is mockery of superstition and sectarianism: Poorgrass kneels and says prayers when a gate won't open and, in the Buck's Head in Troytown, he and Coggan exchange their primitive notions of the differences between church and chapel.[7]

A more serious statement is to be found in the fact that the hero has little time for religion, and in Hardy's comment on the Great Barn, that, unlike the church, it was still used for the purpose for which it was built:

The lanceolate windows, the time-eaten arch-stones and chamfers, the orientation of the axis, the misty chestnut work of the rafters, referred to no exploded fortifying art or worn-out religious creed. The defence and salvation of the body by daily bread is still a study, a religion, and a desire.[8]

The linking of the Gothic style (the '*exploded fortifying art*') to the worn-out religious creed looks forward to the last novel, *Jude the Obscure*, in which alienation from church and medieval art-forms become major themes.

In *The Return of the Native* it is not Christianity but paganism that triumphs on Egdon Heath. Christianity in the novel has its representative in Clym Yeobright. He returns to Egdon from Paris, giving up a successful career as a diamond merchant to set up a school on the heath. Having returned, he is thwarted by Fate, first losing his sight and with it the hope of starting the school, and then his wife, who is drowned in her flight across Egdon to Wildeve. Left alone and friendless in the world, Clym now turns to Christianity and, on the anniversary of his mother's death (we are presumably meant to see it as some sort of atonement), he starts his career as a lay preacher. Merryn Williams makes the point that his blindness is an emblem of his spiritual state. When, at the end of the novel, he looks in at the wedding celebrations of his cousin Thomasin and Diggory Venn, his prime concern is whether the participants are thinking of him, a strangely selfish thought for one who lectures the heath folk on the meaning of the Sermon on the Mount.[9] This cold preacher is indeed a lonely and pathetic figure.

In *Tess of the d'Urbervilles*, instances of cruel religious dogmatism are to be seen in several of the characters. The Clare family and Mercy Chant preach charity but practise cold condemnation. Their sort of charity is seen when Mercy, finding Tess's walking shoes in the ditch, takes them to give to some poor person and Tess is left to limp back to Flintcomb-Ash. Many of the Clare family's religious notions are bound up with social convention and propriety. When Alec d'Urberville has been converted from sinner to evangelist by Angel's father, he takes up a similar religious stance, exhorting and condemning. His sermon in Emminster Barn is '*of the extremist antinomian type: on justification by faith as expounded in the theology of St. Paul*'. St Paul's teachings on sexuality and marriage have often been attacked because of the superior status he gives to virginity and his condemnation of any sexual expression unsanctified by marriage.

Tess's younger sister observes that Earth is a *'blighted star'* and Tess does not contradict her. When she is raped by Alec d'Urberville Hardy comments: *'But where, might some say, where was Tess's guardian angel?'*. Tess's experience in the story as innocent victim of external aggression is directly parallel to that of the wounded pheasants she kills to put them out of their pain, or to the Arctic birds who visit Flintcomb-Ash Farm. She is a migratory wanderer over the earth's surface, uncared for and unprotected by any God. Nor does God's church offer her better treatment. Although Tess has baptized her dying infant with the name Sorrow, he is an unbaptized bastard in the eyes of the Vicar and must be buried

> *in that shabby corner of God's allotment where He lets the nettles grow, and where all unbaptized infants, notorious drunkards, suicides and others of the conjecturally damned are laid.*[10]

The word *'conjecturally'* makes it clear that Hardy cannot conceive of a God who would damn a child for no fault of its own.

In talking to Alec d'Urberville about the fallacies in his evangelical beliefs, Tess explains that although she believes in the spirit of the Sermon on the Mount[9], that is the spirit of love of God and love of neighbour, she cannot accept all she is taught by the Church. Her convictions are based on enquiry *'deep into doctrines'* that she has made with Angel Clare. She presents arguments *'which might possibly have been paralleled in many a work of the pedigree ranging from the* Dictionnaire Philosophique *to Huxley's* Essays'. Appealing to reason rather than to blind faith (as Alec does), her loyalty to Clare and refusal to condemn him show that her charity is genuine. That she should embody for Hardy the ideal of Christian charity was the reason that the novel was greeted with a violent outburst of public indignation. Whilst Hardy must have realized that people would react in that way, it was still deeply hurtful to him when they did.

Tess is a notorious attack on Victorian religious hypocrisy. *Jude the Obscure* raises issues of social and political hypocrisy as well, especially with regard to divorce and education. However, it is the religious issue that shapes the book. The story follows the strange religious progressions of Jude and his cousin, Sue. Jude's initial desire to become a parson is a vain dream, a blazing ideal in the front of his mind. It colours his first view of Sue when he sees her illuminating a religious text. Sue, on the other hand, like Tess in the earlier book, has followed contemporary Biblical scholarship with her student friend. Having rejected traditional religious views (as is seen in her reaction to the map of Jerusalem and by her rearrangement of the books of the Bible), she is veering when we first see her towards a romantic notion of paganism, smuggling statues of Venus and Apollo into her rooms. When Jude suggests that they should visit Melchester cathedral together she says:

> '*Yes. Though I think I'd rather sit in the railway station. .*
> *. . That's the centre of the town life now.*'[11]

In Jude's experience as a stonemason, patching and repairing the stonework of the Christminster Colleges, and in Sue's modernism, Hardy makes a sustained attack on the Gothic style as the artistic equivalent of the backward-looking medievalism of the church. This attack starts with the description of the church at Marygreen. The only remaining relic of local history in the village is a well-shaft. The original church has been pulled down and in its place a

> *new building of modern Gothic design, unfamiliar to English eyes, had been erected on a new piece of ground by a certain obliterator of historic records who had run down from London and back in a day.*[12]

Like the graves in the churchyard the site of the old church has been obliterated. The Church and the University of Christminster are shown to be two imperious social institutions, the one perpetuating an outmoded view of God, the other an outmoded view of education, both out of touch with the individuals they were instituted to serve.

By the end of the novel a complete reversal of religious positions has occurred. Sue's conversion to high-church religious observance is portrayed frankly as a superstitious reaction to the death of her children, and her return to a loveless union with Phillotson because she feels this must be right in the eyes of the Lord, is clearly culpable in human terms. Jude, on the other hand, having been thwarted and rejected at every turn in his career, his marriage and his family, dies with the curse of Job on his lips:

Salisbury Cathedral (Melchester Cathedral in *Jude*): '*I'd rather sit in the railway station . . . That's the centre of town life now.*' (Sue Bridehead in *Jude the Obscure* Pt. 3 Chap. 1 p. 200) (A. F. Kersting)

'*Let the day perish wherein I was born, and the night in which it was said, There is a man child conceived.*'[13]

It is left to the reader to decide which is the more honest reaction to the tragedy of life; but the voice of Jude has always been assumed in essence to be that of Hardy.

What, wrote Hardy's friend Sir Edmund Gosse, *has Providence done to Mr Hardy that he should rise up in the arable land of Wessex and shake his fist at his Creator? . . . we wish he would go back to Egdon and listen to the singing of the heather.*[14]

3. CLASS

Fluctuations of people between classes is a central theme in Hardy's novels. Barriers caused by poor education, low birth or poverty are crossed upwards through superior education (for example, Grace Melbury), inheritance of money (Bathsheba Everdene in *Far from the Madding Crowd* or Lucetta in *The Mayor of Casterbridge*), marriage or simply through skill and diligence (to be seen in Gabriel Oak in *Far from the Madding Crowd* and in Henchard's rise to eminence in Casterbridge). In many of the novels there is also a corresponding sinking, generally through profligacy (such as that of the feckless Durbeyfields in *Tess of the d'Urbervilles*) or misfortune. There are many examples of the latter: Giles Winterborne's loss of his tied cottage in *The Woodlanders*; Gabriel Oak's loss of his invested capital when his dog drives his sheep over a cliff into a marl pit in *Far from the Madding Crowd*; Henchard's loss of his capital through foolish corn-dealing in anticipation of a wet harvest in *The Mayor of Casterbridge*; Clym Yeobright's reduction to furze-cutter when his eyesight goes in *The Return of the Native* and, in *Tess of the d'Urbervilles*, the Durbeyfield loss of any income when their horse Prince dies in an accident. Each blow of fortune brings about an economic change out of which springs the plot's action.

The world of the novels is a class-conscious world at every level of society portrayed. There is little difference in motive between Melbury's desire for his daughter to rise in the world through a boarding-school education (*The Woodlanders*) and Mrs Dewey's reason for upbraiding Reuben for saying '*taties*':

'Well, 'tis what I was never brought up to. With our family
'twas never less than 'taters' and very often 'pertatoes'
outright; mother was so particular and nice with us girls:
there was no family in the parish that kept themselves up more
than we.'[15]

Henchard shows a similar class-conscious fastidiousness in his
attempts to stop Elizabeth-Jane using dialect forms and in his
anger that she should have served at The Three Mariners (*The
Mayor of Casterbridge*).

Fancy Day (*Under the Greenwood Tree*), like Grace Melbury
(*The Woodlanders*), has been educated out of her class. A game-
keeper's daughter, she has been brought up by an aunt and then
gone as a Queen's scholar to training college. Consequently she
feels superior to Dick Dewey. A similar desire resides in Mrs
Yeobright who wants her niece Thomasin *'to look a little
higher than a small dairy-farmer, and marry a professional man'*.[16]
The inferior social status of Diggory Venn, the man who wants
to marry her, is made quite clear. By birth he is son of a
dairyman but he has demeaned himself by becoming a
reddleman, a common tradesman with the additional social
rejection caused by his strange appearance.

Hardy was fascinated enough to trace his own family tree and,
rather dubiously, claimed descent from the le Hardy family of
Jersey. In his claim to be of the same family of Admiral Hardy of
Trafalgar and in his siting of Max Gate on a prominence looking
out towards Hardy's monument we see a snobbish concern with
aristocracy, a desire of the socially unacceptable man to assert his
respectability, that is echoed in the novels.

The aristocratic villain is a figure borrowed straight from
Victorian melodrama. Alec d'Urberville, twirling his moustaches
as he pursues his innocent victims, is the type. Sergeant Troy in
the earlier novel, *Far from the Madding Crowd*, has all the frisson
of aristocratic connections; he is the illegitimate son of Lord
Severn, and his mother had been a French governess. Dr
Fitzpiers in *The Woodlanders* is from *'a very old family, I believe,
the Fitzpiers of Oakbury-Fitzpiers,'*[17] and Lucetta in *The Mayor of
Casterbridge* has a similar background:

*Bath is where my people really belong to, though my
ancestors in Jersey were as good as anybody in England.
They were the Le Sueurs, an old family, who have done
great things in their time.*[18]

Even though most of these characters are either declined aristocrats or, in d'Urberville's case, imposters, they carry the panache of their connections. But it is at the other end of the social scale that we find Hardy's unique contribution to the English novel. His realistic portrayal of farmers, shepherds, timber merchants and the agricultural labourers who together made up English village culture, and his sympathetic description of their problems is something entirely new. He recorded a culture that is now lost but, more important, he gave us a new perspective on the working man as he is acted on by social and economic forces which are beyond his control.

4. PHILOSOPHY

We have already seen, in the first two sections of the chapter, that Hardy's view of God was pessimistic and that he saw Fate as a malevolent force. However, the very novels in which this is evident generally celebrate human qualities of love, fidelity and purity of heart. Of Hardy's replies to the accusation that he was a pessimist, three stand out. The first appears in the poem 'In Tenebris II'. In the first three stanzas he describes the popular, optimistic attitudes to life, and in the third stanza condemns a pessimism that is clearly his own:

> Let him in whose ears the low-voiced Best is killed by the clash of the First,
> Who holds that if way to the Better there be, it exacts a full look at the Worst,
> Who feels that delight is a delicate growth cramped by crookedness, custom, and fear,
> Get him up and be gone as one shaped awry; he disturbs the order here.

The 'clash of the First' reflects Hardy's view that civilization had to progress slowly against the forces of evil and unenlightenment; it is a view that he called evolutionary meliorism. 'The First' is civilization at its earliest and we can progress to 'the Better' only if we examine the full extent of 'the Worst' of human suffering. This is an idea of increasingly civilized behaviour evolving as time progresses, but it does not answer the charge that Hardy sees Fate as a malevolent aggressor.

Nor does his defence, recorded in *Real Conversations*[19]:

> *. . . I believe, indeed, that a good deal of the rumbustious, swaggering optimism of recent literature is at bottom cowardly and insincere . . . my pessimism, if pessimism it be, does not involve the assumption that the world is going to the dogs. . . . On the contrary, my practical philosophy is distinctly meliorist. What are my books but one long plea against 'man's inhumanity to man'—to woman—and to the lower animals? Whatever may be the inherent good or evil of life, it is certain that men make it much worse than it need be.*

Clearly the distinction that we need to draw is between what Hardy claimed to believe personally and the experiences of the characters in his novels.

An example of this is to be found in the 1912 Preface to *Jude the Obscure*. The evolutionary meliorist author is delighted by the foundation of Ruskin College,

> *. . . though I was informed that some readers thought these episodes an attack on venerable institutions, and that when Ruskin College was subsequently founded it should have been called the College of Jude the Obscure.*

But of course the book *is* a bitter attack on Church and University and pessimistic in the extreme. By drawing attention here to an instance of evolutionary meliorism at work in real life, Hardy attempts to hide the pessimism of the fictional work.

When, in 1922, the eighty-two year old Hardy published his book of poems, *Late Lyrics and Earlier*, he was anxious to make his philosophical views quite clear. In 'An Apology' he writes thus:

> *Heine observed nearly a hundred years ago that the soul has her eternal rights; that she will not be darkened by statutes, nor lullabied by the music of bells. And what is to-day, in allusion to the present author's pages, alleged to be 'pessimism' is, in truth, only such 'questionings' in the exploration of reality, and is the first step towards the soul's betterment, and the body's also.*[20]

Here Hardy is justifying pessimism by reference to its moral function and thus claiming to refute the charge. He quotes the line from 'In Tenebris II', '*If way to the Better there be, it exacts a good look at the Worst*', and comments:

> . . . *that is to say, by the exploration of reality, and its*
> *frank recognition stage by stage along the survey, with an*
> *eye to the best consummation possible: briefly, evolutionary*
> *meliorism. But it is called pessimism nevertheless.*

He concludes 'An Apology' with a careful denial of any lack of
belief in man's capacity for betterment. He hopes that there will
be some new alliance between religion

> . . . *which must be retained unless the world is to perish, and*
> *complete rationality . . . by the means of the interfusing*
> *effect of poetry—'the breath and finer spirit of all*
> *knowledge, the impassioned expression of science'.... But*
> *if it be true, as Comte argued, that advance is never*
> *in a straight line, but in a looped orbit, we may, in the*
> *aforesaid moving backward, be doing it* pour mieux sauter,
> *drawing back for a spring. I repeat that I forlornly*
> *hope so, notwithstanding the supercilious regard of hope by*
> *Schopenhauer, von Hartmann, and other philosophers*
> *down to Einstein who have my respect.*[21]

We note that it is a '*forlorn hope*' and when we come to read the
later poems in the collection we are again with the voices of those
who have died unfulfilled, suffering the ironies of chance, living
in lasting grief with only the memories of pleasure past. One does
meet the occasional happy scene, but it is difficult to find much
evidence for Hardy's theory of evolutionary meliorism in either
the novels or the poems. Some poems to consider in this
connection, given with their number in Gibson's edition of *The
Complete Poems*, are: 'A Sign-Seeker' (30); 'The Inpercipient'
(44); 'The Darkling Thrush' (119); 'The Church-Builder' (139);
'A Plaint to Man' (266); 'God's Funeral' (267); 'Aquae Sulis'
(308); 'In A Whispering Gallery' (474); 'A Drizzling Easter
Morning' (620); 'The Graveyard of Dead Creeds' (694) and
'Yuletide In A Younger World' (841).

5. LOVE, MARRIAGE AND DIVORCE

There is a cynicism about romance and marriage in all
of Hardy's novels, but it is only in *The Woodlanders*, *Tess of the
d'Urbervilles* and *Jude the Obscure* that he attempts seriously to
portray the deep unhappiness of ill-matched couples unable to
obtain a divorce. In the early novels, comments about marriage

or the wiles of women are often introduced largely for their humorous effect. Tranter Dewey in *Under the Greenwood Tree* warns his son Dick:

> '*Now, Dick, this is how a maid is. She'll swear she's dying for thee, and she is dying for thee; but she'll fling a look over t'other shoulder at another young feller, though never leave off dying for thee just the same.*'[22]

Dick's view of his own parents' marriage, which might at first be seen as Hardy's view, must be taken in context. After the Christmas party the tranter has suggested that his wife go straight to bed '*or you'll be as white as a sheet in the morning*'.

> *. . . Dick wondered how it was that when people were married they could be so blind to romance; and was quite certain that if ever he took to wife that dear impossible Fancy, he and she would never be so dreadfully practical and undemonstrative of the Passion as his mother and father were. The most extraordinary thing was that all the fathers and mothers he knew were just as undemonstrative as his own.*[23]

At this point we are aware of Dick's innocence rather than of any defect in the relaxed relationship of his parents. More directly cynical is Hardy's observation in *Far from the Madding Crowd*:

> *It appears that ordinary men take wives because possession is not possible without marriage, and that ordinary women accept husbands because marriage is not possible without possession; with totally differing aims the method is the same on both sides.*[24]

At the start of *The Mayor of Casterbridge* when we are shown Henchard and Susan together, Hardy comments that they are clearly man and wife:

> *No other than such relationship would have accounted for the atmosphere of stale familiarity . . .*[25]

However, the emphasis in this novel is on the character of the central figure rather than on marriage as an institution.

When in *The Return of the Native* Thomasin comes back from Anglebury unmarried to Damon Wildeve she makes a comment on the nature of romance which is exemplified in the rest of the novel:

*'I used to think it would be pretty and sweet like that; but
how different!'* Damon replies: *'Yes, real life is never at
all like that.'*[26]

The suggestion that falling in love is romantic illusion finds its
parallels in the educational idealism of Clym and the yearnings of
Eustacia for the bright life away from Egdon Heath. In each case
the grand idea deludes, and reality turns out to be entirely
different and full of unhappiness.

The question of divorce is central to the last three great
novels. Nowadays, when so many marriages end in divorce, we
may forget how difficult this was to obtain in the nineteenth
century. Up to 1858, divorce was a procedure of the
Ecclesiastical Courts and could only be obtained by Act of
Parliament. The Matrimonial Causes Act (1857) established a
Civil Divorce Court. The Act allowed a man to obtain a divorce
if he could establish his wife's adultery; but a woman could
obtain a divorce from her husband only if she could prove
incestuous adultery, bigamy and adultery, rape, sodomy or
bestiality, or adultery coupled with cruelty. When the husband
petitioned, a claim for damages could be instituted against the
correspondent. A decree *nisi* became absolute after six months
and the Court had power to make orders as to the custody,
education and maintenance of the children, alimony and
settlements. The cost of the legal proceedings made divorce the
prerogative of the middle classes.

In *The Mayor of Casterbridge* there is a famous account of
wife-selling, and there is enough evidence to suggest that this
was sometimes used by the working man quite illegally as a
cheap form of divorce. In his *Facts Notebook* Hardy records three
instances of it taken from the *Dorsetshire Chronicle* in the period
1826–29. Roy Palmer in *A Touch of The Times*[27] makes a note to
a song about the sale of a wife:

> *This was not the degrading ordeal which it appears
> however. Normally the marriage had broken down, the sale
> was by common consent, and the purchaser settled in
> advance. Often the parties repaired to a public house to
> celebrate together afterwards and to spend the purchase
> price. . . . The custom of wife-selling provided a form of
> divorce for ordinary people.*

An Oxford social anthropologist, Samuel Menefee, has found

some 200 identifiable instances dating from 1553 to the late nineteenth century. He concludes an article in *New Society*[28]:

> *No more traumatic than most divorce hearings, less expensive than a singles bar, this 'disgusting', 'barbarous', 'outrageous', and 'deplorable' institution—to use only a few of the epithets hurled at it—offered its participants a fresh start in conjugal life.*

But just how widespread and frequent this sensational practice actually was we have little idea. My own guess is that if it was common practice there would be many more instances of prosecutions for wife-selling in nineteenth-century law reports than we have. The case in *The Mayor of Casterbridge* is unusual (and unbelievable) in that the sale was not premeditated and the purchaser was not agreed beforehand.

In *The Woodlanders*, Grace Melbury's failure to obtain a divorce from Fitzpiers was through '*the new statute, twenty and twenty-one Vic.; cap. 85*', that is 1857. However in 1926 Hardy referred to the story's setting as being fifty years ago. It is clear that he has confused the major divorce reform of 1857 with a minor amendment, the Judicature Act of 1878. He intends the story to be set from 1876–79.

In *The Woodlanders*, unlike *Tess* and *Jude*, the unwanted partner in the triangular situation conveniently dies and the estranged husband and wife are re-united; but the tenor of the story is unromantic. Love is seen to blind the intellect and marriage is characterized as sorrowful. Describing Fitzpiers's growing affection for the idea of Grace Melbury, Hardy comments:

> *A young man may dream of an ideal friend likewise, but some humour of the blood will probably lead him to think rather of an ideal mistress, and at length the rustle of a woman's dress, the sound of her voice, or the transit of her form across the field of his vision, will enkindle his soul with a flame that blinds his eyes.*[29]

In Fitzpiers's complex character, with its romanticism on the one hand and its calculating rationalism on the other, there is a good deal of Hardy's own nature. As Grace watches the progress of her husband towards his lover across the autumnal landscape of the White Hart Vale, Hardy comments:

> *In all this proud show some kernels were as unsound as her*
> *own situation, and she wondered if there were one world in*
> *the universe where the fruit had no worm, and marriage no*
> *sorrow.*[30]

Against the implication here that there is no such world, that
unhappiness in marriage follows a universal law as observable in
nature as it is in the human tragedy, must be seen the fidelity of
Marty South whose loving acts enclose the novel.

Tess was a scandalous lady in fiction in several respects. As a
victim of rape she was the mother of an illegitimate child and
tainted by both in the eyes of the Victorian public. But it is after
her marriage to Angel Clare that she becomes something new in
English fiction. A girl whose explicit sexuality has been made
quite clear (she kisses Angel with *'an impassioned woman's kisses'*)
becomes the victim of her husband's sexual repression when he
finds out her secret. When he rejects and leaves her, the reader's
sympathy is strongly with Tess and not with her husband's
rejection of her. What we are faced with is an outright
challenging of Victorian ideas of sexual propriety. But in doing
so Hardy still gives Tess some fairly conventional reactions:

> *Presently she slid down upon her knees beside his foot, and*
> *from this position she crouched in a heap.*[31]

Angel's reaction is unforgiving:

> *He looked upon her as a species of imposter; a guilty*
> *woman in the guise of an innocent one;* but Tess's
> grovelling humility jarrs: *'I shan't ask you to let me live*
> *with you, Angel, because I have no right to!'*[32]

In saying this she is accepting convention's view of a fallen
woman. The section is aptly called 'The Woman Pays', an
epithet appropriate to the role of woman in nineteenth-century
England.

Victorian horror at the idea that the frankly sexual, fallen Tess
should be described in the sub-title as *'A Pure Woman'* had been
violent and immediate. The reaction to *Jude* was even more so.
The Bishop of Wakefield threw his copy onto the fire calling it
'such garbage'; W. H. Smith withdrew it from their lending
libraries and even at his home, as we learn from an anecdote
attributed to Alfred Sutro, Hardy was made to feel the full force
of his sacrilegious attack on the institution of marriage:

There were only he and I and his wife—the first Mrs.
Hardy, of course—at the meal; it was about the time when
Jude The Obscure had been published, and I was loud in
praise of that work. Mrs. Hardy was far from sharing my
enthusiasm. It was the first novel of his, she told me, that he
had published without first letting her read the manuscript:
had she read it, she added firmly, it would not *have been*
published, or at least, not without considerable emendations.
The book had made a difference to them, she added, in the
County . . .[33]

In *Jude the Obscure* the cause of unhappiness in marriage is
that all the participants enter it in a dream world. Arabella is the
least deceived about what she is doing: she is collaring a husband
with prospects. When it turns out that they cannot get on
together, she has the honesty to her emotions to leave Jude. The
dishonesty of her pretended pregnancy pales into insignificance
in comparison with the prevarications of Sue. Jude falls in love
with Sue with the utterly mistaken view that she is a devout
Christian, and she allows it to happen. Having done so, she
accepts the attentions of Phillotson at the same time as
encouraging Jude and, still in a state of indecision, marries him.
Having been granted a divorce from Phillotson and come to live
with Jude, she bears his children. Seeing the death of her
children as divine retribution for her sins, she then seeks solace
in religion, leaves Jude and re-marries Phillotson. At every turn
she lacks honesty to her emotions and in each relationship she
responds to her lover as an object of her own feelings and not as
a separate subject. Hardy sees her as typical of the modern
woman. There is a grain of truth in this for she is freethinking
and liberated from convention, but this portrait of a woman
whose emotions are so undeveloped as to make her incapable of a
mature relationship with anyone is surely an idea out of Hardy's
mind and not, as he puts it in the 1912 Preface:

> *. . . the first delineation in fiction of the woman who was*
> *coming into notice in her thousands every year—the woman*
> *of the feminist movement—the slight, pale, 'bachelor' girl—*
> *the intellectualized, emancipated bundle of nerves that*
> *modern conditions were producing, mainly in cities as yet;*
> *who does not recognize the necessity to follow marriage as a*
> *profession, and boast themselves as superior people because*
> *they are licensed to be loved on the premises.*

There are many assumptions beneath that statement that one would want to question. However, Sue's case in the novel does raise the important issue of the right of a woman over her own body (a right that has not yet been established over the issues of contraception and abortion) when Sue refuses to sleep with her husband, Phillotson. The principle of considerate understanding that Phillotson adopts was by no means widely held to apply in this situation. When he decides to allow Sue to leave him to live with Jude, his friend Gillingham voices the reaction of the respectable Victorian public:

> *'But if people did as you want to do, there'd be a general domestic disintegration. The family would no longer be the social unit.'*[34]

Phillotson's reply anticipates a view only just gaining credence now, some eighty years later: *'And yet, I don't see why the woman and the children should not be the unit without the man.'* This conversation repays careful analysis and consideration.

We are reminded that Hardy's own marriage had reached a period of estrangement and unhappiness when we read his empassioned plea for the exercise of charity in allowing divorce not just for adultery but for incompatibility, the enforced yoke of a loveless marriage. At the beginning of the section 'At Shaston' he quotes Milton's pamphlet *The Doctrine and Discipline of Divorce* (1643), a tract written shortly after the failure of Milton's own disastrous first marriage:

> *Whoso prefers either Matrimony or other Ordinance before the God of Man and the plain Exigence of Charity, let him profess Papist, or Protestant, or what he will, he is no better than a Pharisee.*

An outraged outburst from Mrs Oliphant in *Blackwood's Magazine* (January 1896) called 'The Anti-Marriage League', made the mistake of assuming that Hardy had made an attack on marriage. The novel comes to no conclusions and is, as Hardy points out, as much about the shattering of two people's ideals as it is about marriage. But the veil that had covered the subject of unhappiness in marriage and issues of adult sexuality for so long had been lifted. *Jude the Obscure* asserts these important areas of human experience as proper and vital subjects for fictional treatment.

[1] Thomas Hardy *Tess of the d'Urbervilles* Chap. 59 p. 546   [2] Thomas Hardy *The Mayor of Casterbridge* Chap. 44 p. 403   [3] Thomas Hardy *The Woodlanders* Chap. 3 p. 51   [4] J. Gibson *Thomas Hardy: The Complete Poems* (Macmillan, 1976) 248 'The Convergence of the Twain'   [5] as 3, Chap. 7 p. 90   [6] as 1, Chap. 5 p. 86   [7] Thomas Hardy *Far from the Madding Crowd* Chap. 42 p. 365   [8] *ibid.* Chap. 22 p. 201   [9] Gospel according to St Matthew Chaps. 4–8   [10] as 1, Chap. 14 p. 161   [11] Thomas Hardy *Jude the Obscure* Pt. 3 Chap. 1 p. 200   [12] *ibid.* Pt. 1 Chap. 1 p. 44   [13] *ibid.* Pt. 6 Chap. 11 p. 531   [14] *Cosmopolis*, January 1896   [15] Thomas Hardy *Under the Greenwood Tree* Chap. 8 p. 92   [16] Thomas Hardy *The Return of the Native* Pt. 1 Chap. 9 p. 132   [17] as 3, Chap. 8 p. 100   [18] as 2, Chap. 22 p. 209   [19] William Archer *Real Conversations* (London, 1904) pp. 46 and 47   [20] as 4, p. 557   [21] *ibid.* p. 562   [22] as 15, Chap. 8 p. 149   [23] *ibid.* Chap. 8 p. 95   [24] as 7, Chap. 20 p. 183   [25] as 2, Chap. 1 p. 35   [26] as 16, Bk 1 Chap. 5 p. 89   [27] Roy Palmer (Ed.) *A Touch of the Times* (Penguin, 1974)   [28] *New Society*, 26 January 1978   [29] as 3, Chap. 17 p. 176   [30] *ibid.* Chap. 28 p. 274   [31] as 1, Chap. 35 p. 327   [32] *ibid.* Chap. 35 p. 328   [33] J. R. Sutherland (Ed.) *The Oxford Book of Literary Anecdotes* (O.U.P., 1975)   [34] as 11, Pt. 3 Chap. 4 p. 321.

5

An Introduction to the Poetry

Hardy is a poet's poet and many distinguished poets have recognized their debt to him. Ezra Pound wrote: '*Nobody has taught me anything about writing since Thomas Hardy died*', and again '*Now* there *is clarity. There* is *the harvest of having written 20 novels first.*' In fact many of Hardy's finest poems were written before he stopped writing novels, although it was 1898 before he published his first collection, *Wessex Poems*.

In reading Hardy's poems after, say, the sonorous phrases of Tennyson, it is an immense relief to hear simple phrases and the slight awkwardness of real speech. Though he provided himself with a meticulous training in verse forms, the dominant influences, one feels, are in folk song, the plain strong language of the Book of Common Prayer and the Authorized Version of the Bible with which Hardy lived each day of his life from childhood, and the spoken word of country people. In studying Hardy's poems, poets are drawing on the oral tradition of English verse.

The themes of the poems reflect the concerns of the novels — love, love lost, unfulfilment, grief, memory and the tricks that Time or Fate plays on individuals — but invariably each poem relates to some real occasion in Hardy's life, to a particular place he knows, to a person he has known or to a situation in one of his novels. He once told Clive Holland that there is more autobiographical interest in his poetry than in all his novels.[1] In this poem about his childhood the scene seems to burst on his memory with great visual precision:

'The Self-Unseeing'

Here is the ancient floor
Footworn and hollowed and thin,
Here was the former door
Where the dead feet walked in.

She sat here in her chair,
Smiling into the fire;
He who played stood there,
Bowing it higher and higher.

Childlike, I danced in a dream;
Blessings emblazoned that day;
Everything glowed with a gleam;
Yet we were looking away!

He is writing of his memory of dancing to the tune of his father's fiddle in the cottage at Higher Bockhampton. That his father is now dead and that the position of the front door which used to give entrance straight into the living room has now changed account for the tense change in the third line. In the first and second verses Hardy is recreating the exact moment in the past, a perspective which is altered in the last verse in which we seem to compare the moment of unconscious happiness in childhood with an adulthood from which such joy has gone.

Although it reads so effortlessly, a closer look shows the poet's craftsmanship. Note, for example, the subtle inversion of the '*H*' and '*f*' in the first line into '*F* and '*h*' in the second. A similar musical effect is produced in lines three and four when the first letters of '*former door*' are inverted and echoed in '*dead feet*'. Yet in the last verse the emphatic alliteration of '*danced*' and '*dream*', of '*Blessings*' and '*blazoned*' and '*glowed*' and '*gleam*' recreate the rhythm of the dance. Hardy intended that his poems should be read out loud and that is the best way to hear their rhythms and musical effects. This poem viewing the past from the present is one of many with a dual time perspective. Others referring specifically to his childhood are: 'Night In The Old Home' (222), 'The House of Hospitalities' (156), 'A Church Romance' (211), 'The Fallow Deer At The Lonely House' (551), and 'The Oxen' (403).

The perspective of time often provides Hardy's poems both with their shape and with their distinctive mood. What is too simply labelled as a gloomy view emerges when we examine life in that perspective; after all, human life ends in death; love, all too often, fades, and friends and friendships die. A useful comparison can be made between Keats's 'Ode to A Nightingale' and Hardy's much anthologized poem 'The Darkling Thrush'. Keats is caught in a dream-like state between the misery of life around him, '*Where palsy shakes a few sad last gray hairs*', and the intense experience of beauty in the brief moments in which he is transported by the nightingale's song. Hardy's bird also sings beautifully and moves the poet, but it brings no allaying comfort or compensation for life's emptiness. It is worth observing that Keats's affirmation of beauty in his 'Ode' was written after a re-reading of Shakespeare's *A Midsummer Night's Dream* ('*the musk rose*' and '*the eglantine*' are unconscious borrowings, as is the whole conception of dream versus reality), whereas Hardy's poem is bare of the compensation of art.

'The Darkling Thrush'

I leant upon a coppice gate
When Frost was spectre-gray,
And Winter's dregs made desolate
The weakening eye of day.
The tangled bine-stems scored the sky
Like strings of broken lyres,
And all mankind that haunted nigh
Had sought their household fires.

The land's sharp features seemed to be
The Century's corpse outleant,
His crypt the cloudy canopy,
The wind his death-lament.
The ancient pulse of germ and birth
Was shrunken hard and dry,
And every spirit upon earth
Seemed fervourless as I.

At once a voice arose among
The bleak twigs overhead
In a full-hearted evensong
Of joy illimited ;
An agèd thrush, frail, gaunt and small,
In blast-beruffled plume,
Had chosen thus to fling his soul
Upon the growing gloom.

So little cause for carolings
Of such ecstatic sound
Was written on terrestrial things
Afar or nigh around,
That I could think there trembled through
His happy good-night air
Some blessed Hope, whereof he knew
And I was unaware.

Although mankind is absent from the scene described in the first stanza, human attributes abound. The Frost is *'spectre-gray'* like a ghost; the sinking sun is likened to a weakening eye made desolate, and the bine-stems score the sky, a startling image, for it is usually human flesh that bine-stems score.

In the second stanza, the landscape is likened to the corpse of the Century. It is only in the last two lines that all the human characteristics so far described are carried over to the poet leaning on the gate:

And every spirit upon earth
Seemed fervourless as I.

The visual progression so far has been rather cinematographic. From the gate we have gone to the sky viewed through bine-stems which seem to come into focus. With the mention of mankind having sought their fires we have panned out to the landscape and then the vast expanse of grey cloud in the sighing wind. The contrasting close-up of the shrunken hard and dry ground is followed by the poet. The poem first appeared in the *Graphic* on 29 December 1900, when Hardy was fifty-three, and one naturally imagines his face surveying the death of the old year: a middle-aged man, surveying the grey, frosty landscape as the day dies and seeing in it an image for the death of a bleak century.

These qualities now transfer to the thrush; it is *'frail, gaunt and small, in blast beruffled plume'*. The poem's ending provides us with the contrast between the bird's apparent knowledge of *'some blessed Hope'* (the capital *'H'* suggests that this is a poem about God) and the hopelessness of the poet. That there should be any Hope is dismissed as unlikely in the mind of the poet and is contradicted by all the evidence of landscape, thrush and man.

'The Darkling Thrush' has a regular metre and can easily be set to music. Alliterations such as *'dregs made desolate'*, *'His crypt the cloudy canopy*' and '*growing gloom*' strengthen the rhythms. There are specific echoes of Keats's poem in stanza three, '*Full-hearted*' and '*joy illimited*', but Hardy refuses to be seduced by the song. Just where the texture of the verse is opening out he stops it with the short bathetic words describing the thrush. The poeticality of '*full-hearted evensong*' is blocked by the very ordinary realism of '*An aged thrush, frail, gaunt and small*'.

The word '*outleant*' is one of several words Hardy invented. Whilst it suggests '*layed out*' it echoes the opening words and thus links the poet with the idea of the corpse of the Century. The scene described has become a dramatic externalization of the poet's emotional state.

There are several poems that look at life from the perspective of death. Ghosts and spectres speak from the grave telling us of their lives and of the nature of death. In 'Voices From Things Growing In A Churchyard'² we are addressed by characters from different levels of society who represent youth, beauty or rank. In turn they declare who they were in life—and all are named—and what has now become of them: grass, leaves, berries, a yew, a laurel, withwind and ivy. The verse form is strict and lyrical, each stanza ending:

> *All day cheerily*
> *All night eerily.*

We have here something akin to the medieval Dance of Death that can still be seen painted on the walls of churches and cathedrals: men, women and children from all levels of society are led in a dance by the macabre figure of Death. It is paradoxical that although we see death so often on the television nowadays we have lost the sense of its continuous presence. With our modern literal minds we may find the idea of ghosts talking awkward and old-fashioned, even ridiculous, but there is more in this poem that is literally true than is fictional. Like the Dance of Death paintings the effect is grotesque, funny and yet shocking:

> *And so these maskers breathe to each*
> *Sir or Madam*
> *Who lingers there, and their lively speech*
> *Affords an interpreter much to teach,*
> *As their murmurous accents seem to come*
> *Thence hitheraround in a radiant hum,*
> *All day cheerily,*
> *All night eerily!*²

An example of the medieval Dance of Death (The Fotomas Index)

Other graveyard poems with a similar acceptance of the physical fact of death are: 'Friends Beyond' (36), 'Ah, Are You Digging On My Grave' (269), and 'The Levelled Churchyard' (127). In 'Channel Firing' (247), one of many poems that question Christian doctrine, corpses rise from their graves in the mistaken belief that naval gunnery practice is the last trump calling them to judgment. God, in explaining their error, comments that the world is still as mad as it was when they died:

> *All nations striving to make*
> *Red war yet redder. Mad as hatters*
> *They do no more for Christes sake*
> *Than you who are helpless in such matters.*

The evocation of God's words from the beginning of the medieval morality play *Everyman* when He complains of man's sinfulness before calling Everyman to make his account is followed by another instance of Hardy breaking a firm rhythm with an entirely idiomatic line: '*Than you who are helpless in such matters*'. There is nothing medieval in Hardy's sceptical ending:

> *And many a skeleton shook his head.*
> *'Instead of preaching forty year,'*
> *My neighbour Parson Thirdly said,*
> *'I wish I had stuck to pipes and beer.'*

Again the guns disturbed the hour,
Roaring their readiness to avenge,
As far inland as Stanton Tower,
And Camelot, and Starlit Stonehenge.[3]

The use of names of people and places is as distinctive as that rhythmic inversion in the last line.

Usually the perspective we are given on a situation in the poems is predominantly visual. A scene is observed through particular eyes, as in 'The Fallow Deer At The Lonely House' (551): whilst the deer are on tiptoe trying to peer in, those within are totally unaware of them, an ironic vignette. In 'During Wind And Rain' (441), we are shown four family scenes in three verses: one inside with the family *'singing their dearest songs'*; one outside tidying the garden; one breakfasting on the lawn and one whilst they are moving house with the furniture out on the lawn. The last ironic picture is of rain ploughing down their carved names on gravestones.

A more universal examination of the human tragedy is found in 'At A Lunar Eclipse' (79), one of the few poems that was much anthologized during Hardy's lifetime. Awe is the dominant feeling in the first verse, created by the grandeur of the language and the sense of the immensity of what is happening as the shadow of the earth crosses the moon's surface. Hardy then questions whether he can connect the *'imperturbable serenity'* of the occasion with the real nature of the globe. In verse three he considers the small size of the shade cast by *'Mortality'* on the moon; can man be as insignificant as he appears in this perspective? What he describes as *'Heaven's high human scheme'* in verse three is specified in verse four:

Nations at war with nations, brains that teem,
Heroes, and women fairer than the skies.

In this poem especially, with its scientific outlook and metaphysical twist in the last line, we are aware of the affinity with Donne that Hardy claimed.

Such shifts of visual perspective are frequent in the novels and always have the effect of placing the events in a wider frame of place and time. Clym on Egdon Heath; Tess and Marion crawling over the surface of Farmer Groby's turnip field like flies; the moon reflected in the marl pit when Gabriel Oak has lost his sheep, or the sheep dip seen from above as a Cyclop's

eye; Casterbridge seen from Yalbury Hill as Susan and
Elizabeth-Jane approach it for the first time: in all these
instances the lives of individual human beings are reduced to
something of minute significance. Auden wrote:

> *What I valued most in Hardy then, as I still do, was his*
> *hawk's vision, his way of looking at life from a very great*
> *height....*[4]

Indeed, one of the best ways of understanding this technique in
the novels is to examine some of the associated poems. A student
of *Tess of the d'Urbervilles* would recognize the symbolism of
travelling and movement in the short poem 'The Weary Walker'
(713):

> *A Plain in front of me,*
> *And there's the road*
> *Upon it. Wide country,*
> *And, too, the road.*
>
> *Past the first ridge another,*
> *And still the road*
> *Creeps on. Perhaps no other*
> *Ridge for the road?*
>
> *Ah! Past that ridge a third,*
> *Which still the road*
> *Has to climb furtherward—*
> *The thin white road!*
>
> *Sky seems to end its track;*
> *But no. The road*
> *Trails down the hill at the back.*
> *Ever the road.*

'The Blinded Bird' (375) stands with Tess as the embodiment of
Christian suffering; 'Tess's Lament' (141) draws our attention to
her longing for release from her suffering:

> *I cannot bear my fate as writ,*
> *I'd have my life unbe;*

'The Milkmaid' (126) shares with Tess a oneness with the fertile
impulses of the Var Valley:

The maid breathes words—to vent,
It seems, her sense of Nature's scenery,
Of whose life, sentiment,
And essence, very part is she.

In contrast, 'We Field Women' (866) compares the agonies of chopping swedes and drawing reeds with the idyll of the summer at Talbothays. 'Heredity' (363) is concerned with the family face and may be seen as comment on the faces at Woolbridge Manor in which Tess could discern her own features in exaggerated form. 'The Lost Pyx' (140) tells the legend of Cross-in-Hand where Tess met Alec, and 'Beyond The Last Lamp' (257) expands a comment Hardy makes on a stranger's view of the two estranged lovers walking by the banks of the Froom.[5] Some of these fictional situations have just as much emotional realism in Hardy's mind as events that relate to his own life.

The series of poems 'Veteris Vestigia Flammae' (the relics of the old flame), written after the death of Emma in 1912, recreates the days of their courtship on the coast of north Cornwall, placing that early passion against the divisions that time and the inescapable fact of death have brought. This contrast can be seen in the first and last verses of 'Beeny Cliff March 1870—March 1913' (291):

I

O the Opal and the sapphire of that wandering western sea,
And the woman riding high above with bright hair flapping
free—
The woman whom I loved so, and who loyally loved me.

V

What if still in chasmal beauty looms that wild weird
western shore,
The woman now is—elsewhere—whom the ambling pony
bore,
And nor knows nor cares for Beeny, and will laugh there
nevermore.

In 1913 the poet revisited the scenes which held special significance in his courtship. A poem called 'At Castle Boterel' recounts one such visit. Coming to a particular spot, the junction of a lane and highway, Hardy recalls a conversation he had with Emma at the same spot long ago as they had walked alongside their pony and chaise to lighten its load:

Beeny Cliff, a sketch by Hardy made during his courtship of Emma Gifford (by courtesy of Dorset Museum and the Trustees of the Thomas Hardy Memorial Collection). The following words from 'The Figure in the Scene', a poem which appears in *Moments of Vision*, recapture the scene:

> "I stood back that I might pencil it
> With her amid the scene;
> Till it gloomed and rained."

What we did as we climbed, and what we talked of
Matters not much, nor to what it led,—
Something that life will not be balked of
Without rude reason till hope is dead,
And feeling fled.[6]

The assertion of the timeless worth of love is made here against the background of the primeval cliffs and the irony of the entire situation. The last verse leaves us a picture of a sad man vowing never again to visit the former haunts of his dead love. Journeys are found in many poems and novels with a symbolic strength, a mythic equivalent for the search of the isolated individual for some sort of peace, security or fulfilment. This actual pilgrimage to Cornwall had a similar personal significance to the poet. A statement about young love and its significance is made in the simpler poem 'In Time of The Breaking of Nations' (500):

I

Only a man harrowing clods
In a slow silent walk
With an old horse that stumbles and nods
Half asleep as they stalk.

II

Only a thin smoke without flame
From the heaps of couch-grass;
Yet this will go onward the same
Though Dynasties pass.

III

Yonder a maid and her wight
Come whispering by:
War's annals will cloud into night
Ere their story die.

Although the poem was written in 1915 he tells us that the poem '*contains a feeling that moved me in 1870, during the Franco-Prussian war, when I chanced to be looking at an agricultural incident in Cornwall*'. As a man Hardy had this strange ability to keep hidden within him for years deep emotions which would then erupt; just how difficult this made him as a man to live with is made clear in the second volume of Robert Gittings' biographical study, *The Older Thomas Hardy*.

Poems other than those he wrote about Emma seem to record moments of an autobiographical nature. 'Neutral Tones' (9) records a meeting with a girl by a pond (probably Rushy Pond on the heathland above the cottage), at which bitter words were exchanged which the poet, now with hindsight, sees as emblematic of the deception in love that was to follow. The feelings and setting are completely merged and the '*Frost's decree*' which '*unblooms the best hope ever sown*' carries the annual death in the natural world into the emotional sphere. Pinion compares this parallelism with Hardy's imagery in *The Wood-landers* at the point when Marty South's hopes of gaining Giles's love have gone:

*The bleared white visage of a sunless winter day emerged
like a dead-born child.*[7]

When in the poems there is no such merging, as for example in 'A
Broken Appointment' (99), the experience described seems more
trivial and the thought more egocentric.

One of Hardy's favourite poems was a ballad he wrote called
'A Trampwoman's Tragedy' (153). Apart from the rhythmic
power, alliteration, rhyme and use of repetition which are the
ballad's stylistic features, Hardy has an intuitive grasp of the
significance of natural symbols: the tree, the sun, and the
moonshine:

XII
And in the night as I lay weak,
As I lay weak,
The leaves a-falling on my cheek,
The red moon low declined—
The ghost of him I'd die to kiss
Rose up and said: 'Ah, tell me this!
Was the child mine, or was it his?
Speak, that rest I may find!'

Place names are also prominent in the poem, marking out the
course of the fateful journey. When in the ballad's conclusion the
speaker has told the ghost of her murdered lover that he was the
father of her child, she is left alone in life *'haunting the Western
Moor'*. We are conscious of the particularity of the events, for
example through the place names, and at one and the same time
our distance from them—it is a story of something that happened
long ago.

In such ballads we see the novelist and countryman's love of
story. Indeed in many of the poems we return to the qualities of
the young Hardy: his eye for visual detail, his sense of isolation
within the environment, his affection for the past and, as much in
subject matter as in the lyrical verse forms, his love of music.
Already, in 'The Self-Unseeing' (135), we have seen that Hardy
associates music with his childhood and, in that poem, the secure
relationship of mother, father and son. But, as in many of his
musical poems, the relationship is something of the past. In 'A
Church Romance' (211) he recalls his mother looking up to the
gallery in Mellstock and seeing his father:

> *One strenuous viol's inspirer seemed to throw*
> *A message from his string to her below,*
> *Which said: 'I claim thee as my own forthright.'*

Having recalled the romance he places it carefully in the perspectives of time and memory:

> *Thus their hearts' bond, in due time signed.*
> *And long years hence, when Age had scared Romance,*
> *At some old attitude of his or glance*
> *That gallery scene would break upon her mind,*
> *With him as minstrel, ardent, young and trim,*
> *Bowing 'New Sabbath' or 'Mount Ephraim'.*

The harmony of the scene is human as well as musical. Other poems in which he uses music centrally are: 'One We Knew' (227), 'The House of Hospitalities' (156), 'Afternoon Service at Mellstock' (356), 'To My Father's Violin' (381), 'Silences' (849), 'Lost Love' (259), 'A Duettist to Her Pianoforte' (543), and 'The Choirmaster's Burial' (489).

A similar affection for country dance is evident but invariably the dance is used, as it is in the novels, as a metaphor for changing partnerships in love. Dances, journeys, constantly shifting visual perspectives: these are characteristic of Hardy's resistance to portraying human beings in any state of stasis.

The fascination that Hardy had for form, evident as much in his musical interests as in his architectural training, can be seen in the variety of the verse forms he uses and invents. Auden, acknowledging a considerable debt to Hardy, comments:

> *no English poet, not even Donne or Browning, employed so*
> *many and so complicated stanza forms.*[4]

Many of these forms approximate to the simple hymn metres he knew from his youth but he rarely stays strictly within the regular metre. Often the voice of ordinary speech works against the metrical rhythm as in the line *'Which said: 'I claim thee as my own forthright''* ('A Church Romance'). Florence Hardy comments that he recognized the value of *'cunning irregularity'*.

Those who see Hardy only as a melancholy poet should read 'Great Things' (414) or 'Weathers' (512), a song that learns much from Shakespeare. But these poems are typical only in the particularity of their visual detail. More characteristic is the last poem in *Moments of Vision* (1917), in which he imagines what people might say about him when he is dead. Although the poem celebrates the poet's response to the natural world, the fact of death echoes through it—the latching door, the hawk-moth (traditionally representative of the human soul) and the funeral bell. For Hardy, the detail of the world he observed spoke to him of his own place in it, and his own response to the living environment involved an awareness of his own mortality:

> *When the Present has latched its postern behind my*
> *tremulous stay,*
> *And the May moth flaps its glad green leaves like wings,*
> *Delicate-filmed as new-spun silk, will the neighbours say,*
> *'He was a man who used to notice such things'?*
>
> *If it be in the dusk when, like an eyelid's soundless blink,*
> *The dewfall-hawk comes crossing the shades to alight*
> *Upon the wind-warped upland thorn, a gazer may think,*
> *'To him this must have been a familiar sight..'*
>
> *If I pass during some nocturnal blackness, mothy and warm,*
> *When the hedgehog travels furtively over the lawn,*
> *One may say, 'He strove that such innocent creatures should*
> *come to no harm,*
> *But he could do little for them; and now he is gone.'*
>
> *If, when hearing that I have been stilled at last, they stand at the*
> *door,*
> *Watching the full-starred heavens that winter sees,*
> *Will this thought rise on those who will meet my face no more,*
> *'He was one of those who had an eye for such mysteries'?*
>
> *And will any say when my bell of quittance is heard in the gloom,*
> *And a crossing breeze cuts a pause in its outrollings,*
> *Till they rise again, as they were a new bell's boom,*
> *'He hears it not now, but used to notice such things'?*[8]

N.B. All poems cited in this chapter are given with their number as they appear in J. Gibson *Thomas Hardy: The Complete Poems* (Macmillan, 1976)

[1] Clive Holland *Thomas Hardy O. M.* (Herbert Jenkins, 1933) Chap. 6   [2] J. Gibson *Thomas Hardy: The Complete Poems* (Macmillan, 1976) 580 'Voices From Things Growing in a Churchyard'   [3] *ibid.* 247 'Channel Firing'   [4] W. H. Auden 'A Literary Transference', reprinted in A. J. Guerard (Ed.) *Hardy: A Collection of Critical Essays* (Prentice-Hall, 1963)   [5] Thomas Hardy *Tess of the d'Urbervilles* p. 333   [6] as 2, 292 'At Castle Boterel'   [7] Thomas Hardy *The Woodlanders* Chap. 4   [8] as 2, 511 'Afterwards'

6

An Introduction to Seven Novels

UNDER THE GREENWOOD TREE (1872)

> *Under the greenwood tree*
> *Who loves to lie with me*
> *And turn his merry note*
> *Unto the sweet bird's throat,*
> *Come hither, come hither, come hither:*
> > *Here shall he see*
> > *No enemy*
> *But winter and rough weather.*[1]

Shakespeare's song suggests a life of love and idyllic ease in the Forest of Arden. This mood of delightful pastoral is also the dominant mood of Hardy's novel. It is a tale of love among country folk who live in harmony with their surroundings and it ends with a marriage and celebration. Song, dance and music are never far away and help to suggest the harmonious pattern in the events described as the story follows them through the seasons to which they correspond. The world we are in seems timeless; it is a tableau of happy, good-humoured, rustic life, delicately drawn and full of detail, and the book's sub-title shows that this was Hardy's intention: 'The Mellstock quire: a rural painting of the Dutch School'. Certainly it lacks the deep pessimism and anguish of the later novels but it does share some of their themes. This gentle lament for a harmonious life now past has strong realistic elements.

Consider the character of Fancy Day. Educated out of contentment with her lot, she flirtatiously wavers between Farmer Shiner, Parson Maybold and the ingenuous Dick Dewey, the son of the tranter. In chapter five of the 'Autumn' section Dick Dewey calls in on Fancy on his way to assist at the funeral of a friend in a nearby village:

> *she had actually donned a hat and feather and lowered her hitherto plainly looped-up hair, which now fell about her shoulders in a profusion of curls.*[2]

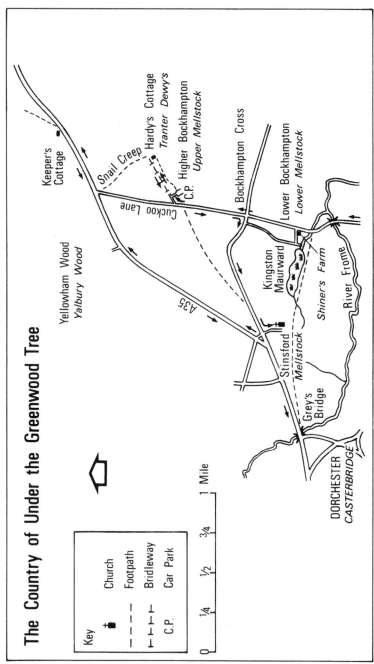

Map, *Under the Greenwood Tree*

This is the day that she is going to play for the first time the organ that has supplanted the old string choir. Dick is shocked that she should dress so strikingly on a day he will be absent from church; she placates him with a kiss and an invitation to visit her tomorrow. At the service she attracts the loving attention of Maybold: '*he admired her during that sermon time as he had never loved a woman before*'. At the end of that afternoon she sits at her window and sees Dick returning from the funeral. Some japanning from his friend's coffin has rubbed off on his coat but he is unperturbed by this and comments to Fancy:

> '*I don't care about that, for 'twas the last deed I could do for him; and 'tis hard if you can't afford a coat for an old friend.*'[3]

In contrast, Fancy will not lean out of the window to kiss him lest her hair get wet, and so in the one picture we see his loyalty and her vanity. In Fancy Day we have the forerunner of Bathsheba Everdene, Grace Melbury and Sue Bridehead: all women who cause unhappiness to others through their vanity and emotional vacillation. Neither is Fancy's marriage to Dick in the last chapter without foreboding. The nightingale sings and the chapter's title warns of unhappiness. It is taken from a song by Thomas Campbell (1774–1844):

> *Can you keep the bee from ranging,*
> *Or the ringdove's neck from changing?*
> *No! Nor fettered love from dying*
> *In the knot there's no untying.*

The Mellstock church '*quire*' is based on the Stinsford church choir in which Hardy's father and grandfather played. Thomas Hardy senior played violincello (William Dewey's part); Thomas Hardy junior played tenor viol (Reuben Dewey's part); James Hardy played treble violin (Dick Dewey's part) and James Dart played second violin (Michael Mail's part). Although the Stinsford string choir ceased playing before Hardy could have joined them, we have only to glance at the *Life* to see his strong affection for the settings of hymns and psalms he had learnt as a boy. Pinion has an excellent section on this in *A Hardy Companion*.[4] The making of the music is predominantly a social activity and the meeting in the tranter's house, the Christmas party and carol singing are all based on childhood memories of actual events. William Dewey, as head of the Dewey family and leader of the quire, has a particular strength and authority on most matters (especially cider and music), and one assumes that Hardy had the figure of his grandfather in his mind's eye. However, these rustic characters are not portrayed realistically: they belong to a literary convention which stretches back to the rustics in *A Midsummer Night's Dream* and beyond. They are excellent and honest souls but they are there for humorous effect. That is not to say that we laugh at them. We do laugh at things they say (*'Marrying a woman is a thing you can do at any moment; but a swarm of bees won't come for the asking'*, says Dick Dewey arriving late for his wedding; a dead Mellstock man is described as *'good, but not religious good'*) and at some of the things they do (for example, at the hilarious interview with Parson Maybold), but we are never invited to mock them and each is characterized individually. One of their functions is to provide a constant against which we can judge the behaviour of Maybold, Shiner and Fancy. Between the members of the quire is a delicacy of relationship which is based on acceptance of each other as individuals and a certain gentleness. It is evident in their attitude to Leaf (they accept him and include him) and in their patient resignation to their dismissal. Their humility shows up Fancy's vanity; their practical skills and proverbial wisdom make Fancy's education appear skin-deep; and the continuity of experience that the three generations of the Dewey family represent makes the antics of the young lovers seem as but one movement in a continuous dance in time. There is the same feeling of continuity down the generations when Mr Penny sees the family foot in Fancy Day's shoe. The feeling persists to the last chapter when the whole village walks the newly-weds round the parish on White Sunday.

Themes which are developed more fully in later and more bitter novels are subsumed within the harmony of the idyll. Class-consciousness and the alienating effect of a superior education are found in Keeper Day's second wife and in Fancy herself. There is also some feeling of the idea that there is a principle of cruelty that permeates all of nature. One instance of this is the point at which Dick Dewey has broached the question of his marriage to Fancy with Keeper Day:

> *Dick said nothing; and the stillness was disturbed only by some small bird that was being killed by an owl in the adjoining wood, whose cry passed into the silence without mingling with it.*[5]

In the very next chapter the build-up to Fancy's visit to Elizabeth Endorfield is achieved through a heavily anthropomorphic description of the woods:

> *A single vast grey cloud covered the country, from which the small rain and mist had just begun to blow down in wavy sheets, alternately thick and thin. The trees of the fields and plantations writhed like miserable men as the air wound its way swiftly among them. . . .*[6]

The passage continues describing the sufferings of the wood, but whereas in *Tess* we would link a similar description to the sufferings of the heroine in a tragic world, here it appears as background music for the '*Deep Body*', Elizabeth Endorfield, who gives Fancy her remedy so that the book may end in the lovers' coming together in marriage.

There is a calm, a sense of peace and community in this book which we do not meet again in Hardy's novels.

FAR FROM THE MADDING CROWD (1874)

Following the success of the rustic portrait in *Under the Greenwood Tree*, Hardy again takes a line from a poem (Gray's 'Elegy in A Country Churchyard') as title and produces another picture of retired country life. The Mellstock community has its parallel in the workfolk sitting round the fire in Warren's Malthouse or sheep-shearing in the Great Barn. But against this pastoral setting are placed characters who are complex in comparison with the simple types of the earlier novel.

Boldwood is close to Parson Maybold in more than name; he is a man with a hard exterior of self-sufficiency that hides a whirlpool of emotion within. His melancholy on being rejected by Bathsheba points forward to the dark moods of Michael Henchard in *The Mayor of Casterbridge*.

Bathsheba, vain and vacillating between her three admirers, is a development from Fancy Day, but she has a sexual vibrancy that only Troy can fully respond to. The girl who gets her skirt tangled in Troy's spur and who places her body at the centre of his sword-drill—two highly charged metaphoric scenes—is very different from the chastened and experienced lady who eventually marries the Laodicean and loyal Gabriel Oak. In Bathsheba's sexuality Hardy raises issues which are to receive fuller treatment in the contrasts between Angel and Alec in *Tess of the d'Urbervilles* and Sue and Arabella in *Jude the Obscure*.

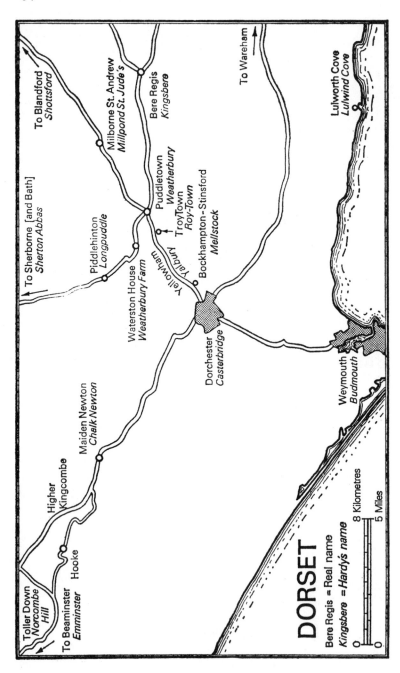

Map, *Far from the Madding Crowd* (Macmillan Publishers, Ltd)

Unlike Dick Dewey, Oak is not a simple rustic at the mercy of the whims of his love, though he does share Dick's loyalty. Gabriel is a pragmatist, skilled, hard-working, self-educated and not to be ruled either by Fate or a woman. The man who rescues Bathsheba's ricks twice, who tells her plainly what he thinks of her flirtation with Boldwood, who will not come to relieve the blasted sheep until he is asked properly, combines admirable personal qualities with proved practical abilities and strong emotions.

There are various indications that Hardy intended to raise this rustic story above the level of literary sketching to the status of high tragedy. At the side of Fanny Robin's coffin when Frank Troy turns away from his wife to his dead love, Bathsheba's anguish is described thus:

> *At these words there arose from Bathsheba's lips a long, low cry of measureless despair and indignation, such a wail of anguish as had never before been heard within these old-inhabited walls. It was the* τετελεσται *of her union with Troy.*[7]

The Greek word means 'It is finished' and was Christ's penultimate cry upon the Cross.

That the individual events are part of wider processes in time is felt especially at the moment Oak grasps what has happened to his sheep:

> *Oak raised his head, and wondering what he could do, listlessly surveyed the scene. By the outer margin of the pit was an oval pond, and over it hung the attenuated skeleton of a chrome yellow moon, which had only a few days to last — the morning star dogging her on the left hand. The pool glittered like a dead man's eye, and as the world awoke a breeze blew, shaking and elongating the reflection of the moon without breaking it, and turning the image of the star to a phosphoric streak upon the water. All this Oak saw and remembered.*[8]

When Troy sees the effect of the spouting gurgoyle on Fanny's grave Hardy says that he saw a *'pitiless anathema'* (or curse of the Gods) written in the *'spoliated effort of his new born solicitousness'*. He sees himself a victim of Providence:

> *... but to find that Providence, far from helping him into a new course, or showing any wish that he might adopt one, actually jeered his first trembling and critical attempt in that kind, was more than nature could bear.*[9]

One of the functions of the rustics is similar to that of the Chorus in a Greek tragedy, to comment on the action and relate it to recurrent processes. However, Troy's experience of helplessness in the face of nemesis is not the dominant mood of the book. The regenerative force of Oak's love matched by the strong evocation of nature's growth suggests that man's life need not be tragic.

Stylistically, *Far from the Madding Crowd* is occasionally pretentious, especially in the metaphors taken from art. When Bathsheba realizes that Oak has seen her leaning back in the saddle she blushes:

> *From the Maiden's Blush, through all varieties of the Provence down to the Crimson Tuscany the countenance of Oak's acquaintance quickly graduated ...*[10]

The colour of the coat of Gabriel's dog is described thus:

> *... but the grey, after years of sun and rain, had been scorched and washed out of the more prominent locks, leaving them of a reddish-brown, as if the blue component of the grey had faded, like the indigo from the same kind of colour in Turner's pictures.*[11]

Of Liddy Smallbury's complexion we are told:

> *The beauty her features might have lacked in form was amply made up for by perfection of hue, which at this winter-time was the softened ruddiness on a surface of high rotundity that we meet with in a Terburg or a Gerard Douw ...*[12]

Grinding the shears, Oak raises Bathsheba's complexion to an angry blush '*with the angry crimson of a Danby sunset*',[13] and Troy awakes in Weatherbury churchyard to see the leaves

> *now sparkling and varnished by the raindrops to the brightness of similar effects in the landscapes of Ruysdael and Hobbema ...*[14]

But these examples are scattered and obtrude little. The

awkwardness of style in the passage describing Fanny's dying crawl up Casterbridge High Street to the Workhouse is a different thing: it demands careful study, for here the style is powerfully expressive of Fanny's painful efforts.

The artist's eye is never more evident than in this novel. It is seen in the building-up of *tableaux vivantes* that externalize the feelings of the people within them: Bathsheba, symbolically red-jacketed and lit up by the sun, blushing as she examines herself in the looking-glass; Oak in the two stackyard scenes; Troy's first encounter with Bathsheba in the plantation; Fanny standing in the snow outside Troy's barracks; the scene by the side of Fanny's coffin lit by the one candle; the malignant swamp by which Bathsheba awakes the next morning. More complex is Hardy's confident use of contrasts between the very near and the very far; between light and darkness and different colours; and between the thing observed and the position of the observer. The scene in which Gabriel is dipping sheep and Boldwold appears is one of many examples of the way in which Hardy's manipulation of our visual perspectives enacts the feelings and tensions within the scene.

There are small weaknesses of plot, such as Fanny going to the wrong church or Troy reappearing as Dick Turpin, that stretch credulity, and the hastily written last chapters lack the power of the rest of the novel. But this novel has a freshness and response to a regenerative natural world (of which the sexuality of Bathsheba and Troy is a part) that is its unique appeal. One is aware that it grows out of the experience that it celebrates, that of young love.

THE RETURN OF THE NATIVE (1878)

The heath behind his cottage that Hardy knew as a boy is very small, nothing like as grandiose as the mythical Egdon Heath that he has made out of it, but we must remember that the eyes of a child transform physical landscape, infusing it with feeling and association. Much of what we see in the novel, even if not actually viewed through the eyes of a child, has that sort of emotion and closeness: Charley's sights of the reddleman; Wildeve and Venn dicing by the light of glow-worms and suddenly disturbed by heath-croppers; or simply the description of the wind scouring the dried heath-bells. Memories of Napoleon such as Hardy might have heard from his grand-

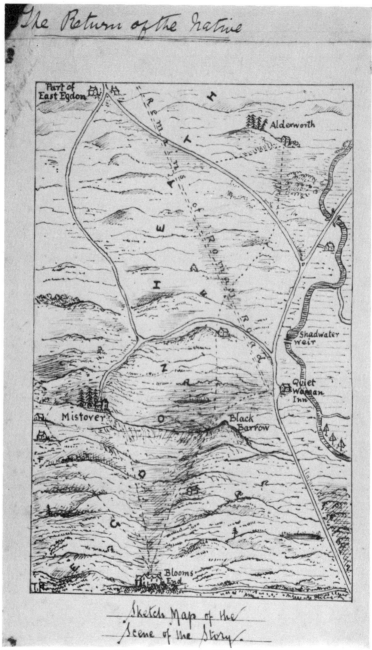

Map, *The Return of the Native* (by courtesy of Dorset County Museum and the Trustees of the Thomas Hardy Memorial Collection)

mother; Christmas mumming and the Christmas party at Blooms
End; and indeed the theme of a mother's love for her son which
is unique to this novel among Hardy's work all reflect Hardy's
childhood experience.

Similarly, the time scale to which the heath reduces human
affairs, though it is partly historical and partly geological, reflects
the suspension of time that appears to occur when we think back
to the seemingly endless days of childhood play:

> *To do things musingly, and by small degrees, seemed, indeed*
> *to be a duty in the Egdon valleys at this transitional hour,*
> *for there was that in the condition of the heath itself which*
> *resembled protracted and halting dubiousness. It was the*
> *quality of repose appertaining to the scene. This was not the*
> *repose of actual stagnation, but the apparent repose of*
> *incredible slowness.*[15]

Though the emotional sources of the story lie in Hardy's
childhood, he very consciously tries to charge it with the
significance and status of tragedy. In the early chapters leading
up to chapter seven, 'Queen of Night', Hardy builds up
associations with the heath, with the bonfires and finally with the
character of Eustacia, which stretch in one direction towards
mythology (especially of the Promethean struggle for survival)
and in the other towards Greek tragedy. The way this is done is
complex. Sometimes it is by direct simile and allusion but more
often with a tongue-in-cheek irony which leaves the reader
unsure whether the allusion is intended entirely seriously. For
example, in the description of Eustacia in 'Queen of Night', we
waver between the perspective of a casual observer, that of the
author, and that of Eustacia's view of herself. The method is
more subtle than is generally allowed by critics of these opening
chapters.

The setting of the heath and the idea of witchcraft (in Hardy's
original plans Eustacia was to have been a witch, *'and more*
malevolently a persecutor of a helpless Thomasin Yeobright than she
now is'[16]) owe something to Shakespeare's *Macbeth*, and Eustacia
has something of Lady Macbeth's ruthless ambition. Clym, alone
on a heath that echoes his isolation, is reminiscent both of
Shakespeare's King Lear and Sophocles' Oedipus, who atoned
for killing his father and marrying his mother by blinding
himself. The heath is more successful as a tragic component than
any individual character. It teems with life (butterflies, snakes,

rabbits, glow-worms and those ponies Hardy calls heath-croppers which suggest something more on the scale of Dartmoor rather than the sandy scrub-land stretching east from his birthplace), and contains the life impulses of the November bonfires, the gypsying and the May dance, but it also brings death to Mrs Yeobright, Wildeve and Eustacia. Clym, in goggles and leather leggings, it reduces to *'a brown spot in the midst of an expanse of olive-green gorse and nothing more'*. By careful insistence Hardy builds up a picture of the heath as the equivalent in the physical world of the experience of the characters:

> *It was at present a place perfectly accordant with man's nature—neither ghastly, hateful, nor ugly: neither commonplace, unmeaning, nor tame; but, like man, slighted and enduring; and withal singularly colossal and mysterious in its swarthy monotony.*[17]

Within this setting, the dance of human relationships portrayed is presented as being tragic: the three protagonists, Eustacia, Wildeve and Clym are incapable of fulfilled human relationships and are driven towards self-destruction by the obsessive pursuit of a personal ideal—but individually none of them attains the sort of status we afford to a tragic hero. They are too petty.

Eustacia's yearning for the distant, whether it be for Paris or the mysterious jewel-dealer who is returning to the heath, is her driving force. It finds its parallel impulse in Clym's idealism, his intention to bring education to the heath folk and later, pathetically, religion. In their courtship and marriage each is in pursuit of a consuming ideal. On Rainbarrow, beneath the moon, symbol of the distant and unobtainable ideal, they declare their love.

But what is Eustacia's yearning other than a failure to relate to her immediate environment, a failing that destroys her marriage? And what is Clym's idealism if not a failure to live away from home, to break the birth-cord that holds him to his mother? Eustacia dies in pursuit of new love, and Clym lives on, preaching abstractions and incapable of relationships. His living emotions having died with Mrs Yeobright, his preaching is an atonement for his feelings of guilt.

Wildeve shares a personal restlessness with Eustacia and Clym. But whereas Clym seems putty in Eustacia's hand and lacking in directive masculinity, Wildeve is passionate. At the gypsying Eustacia and Wildeve respond to the dance with a pagan physicality; their response to each other is instinctual and a sort of self-gratification:

> ... the pride of life was all in all, and they adored none other than themselves.[18]

But this sexuality is also less than heroic. Eustacia idealizes Wildeve during her spare hours '*for want of a better object*' and when Wildeve taunts her he admits the shallowness of his own emotional response:

> '*However the curse of inflammability is upon me, and I must live under it, and take any snub from a woman. It has brought me down from engineering to innkeeping . . .*'[19]

Wildeve's signal, the moth in the flame, is entirely appropriate to his nature: it echoes the signal fire lit for Eustacia which draws him to his destruction.

One would like to find greater heroism in the idealism of Clym or in the mother love of Mrs Yeobright. But the former is cold and selfish and the latter motivated by a possessiveness that is obsessional. She sees herself as '*a broken-hearted woman cast off by her son*'.

We first see Thomasin, dejected and worn out, in the back of Diggory's waggon, a weak woman, victim of her own silly mistake over the licences. Of her later married life with Wildeve we see very little. Lacking the sexuality of Tess in the later novel, she shares with her the imagery of birds. In Book Three, 'The Fascination', we first see Clym travelling across the heath to the new cottage beyond East Egdon. There are many symbolic suggestions of the suffering he is causing by leaving his mother and cousin. The beeches are being torn under the weight of their new leaves in the gale and in

> a neighbouring brake a finch was trying to sing; but the wind blew under his feathers till they stood on end, twisted round his little tail . . .[20]

Later in the chapter, in the afternoon of the day that Clym has left, Thomasin visits Mrs Yeobright for the first time since her marriage:

> *In her movements, in her gaze, she reminded the beholder of the feathered creatures that lived around her home. All*

similes and allegories concerning her began and ended with birds. There was as much variety in her motion as in their flight. When she was musing she was a kestrel, which hangs in the air by an invisible motion of its wings. When she was in a high wind her light body was blown against trees and banks like a heron's. When she was frightened she darted noiselessly like a kingfisher. When she was serene she skimmed like a swallow, and that is how she was moving now.[21]

On the morning that Clym, her cousin, marries Eustacia Vye, a sparrow flies into Mrs Yeobright's kitchen and is trapped. We immediately connect that sparrow with Thomasin:

This roused the lonely sitter who got up and released the bird, and went to the door. She was expecting Thomasin . . .[22]

But like this bird (and unlike Tess) Thomasin escapes death. She has a child, and the story ends with her marriage to Venn. Victim she may be, but she rises to no height of tragic proportion.

The heath folk, as distinctively characterized as their counterparts in *Far from the Madding Crowd*, seem to grow out of the heath when they first appear in chapter three: the lively Granfer Cantle with his memories of 1804; his youngest son, Christian, born when there was no moon, whom no woman will marry; Timothy Fairway, who dances a jig in the embers of the fire with the well-favoured but '*noisily-constructed*' Susan Nunsuch. In the novel they provide comic relief, comment and information. In them we see an acceptance of their lot in life (for example, Christian Cantle's acceptance of his own timidity and the fact that he will never marry) which is so patently absent in Wildeve, Clym, Eustacia and Mrs Yeobright. When we see them, they are invariably about some celebration of life, whether this be the seasonal festivals, greeting Wildeve and Thomasin back from their supposed marriage, mumming or simply stuffing a bed for the couple as at the end of the book. Our last glimpse of them is through Thomasin's window, raising their glasses to drink the health of the newly weds.

Diggory Venn has a similar closeness to the heath. Young Charley is not the only one who feels that this wanderer, stained red with his trade, his eye '*keen as that of a bird of prey and blue as autumn mist*' has some preternatural power. His silence, established first when he walks alongside Captain Vye, and his ability to appear noiselessly as if from nowhere whenever the plot requires him, suggests to the reader some strange spirit of the heath. Nowhere is this more compelling than in the description of the dicing for Mrs Yeobright's money by the light of glow-worms. The heath-croppers, the death's-head moth that extinguishes the candle, and even the glow-worms excite Wildeve's anger as Diggory quietly plays on. The opening description of the heath perfectly describes Diggory, who embodies its power: *'the storm was its lover, and the wind its friend'*; *'untameable Ishmaelite thing'*; *'In its venerable one coat lay a certain satire on human vanity in clothes'*; *'like man, slighted and enduring'*. The book's ending is perfectly accordant with this characterization; though slighted by fortune earlier in the story, Diggory endures and eventually (like Oak in *Far from the Madding Crowd*) marries his love. Had Hardy had serious doubts about the artistic honesty of the ending he would surely have changed it in some later edition of the book.

The Return of the Native is a strong but flawed novel. None of the characters comes up to the tragic stature we are led to expect, and the plot rests on some extraordinary coincidences and unlikely events. Its strength lies in the power of coherence between character and environment. The symbolic settings in the other novels are invariably counterbalanced by some other contrasting place—Talbothays, the idyllic dairy farm in *Tess of the d'Urbervilles*, is matched by the starve-acre Flintcomb-Ash. Egdon stands alone in English literature, combining at one and the same time all the impulses and processes of natural life and an indifference to that life. Out of the rough heath land on which he played as a boy, Hardy has created a fictional setting that is his strongest statement of his view of life.

THE WOODLANDERS (1887)

There is a process of depersonalization of the individual in *The Woodlanders* which extends beyond the fates of Giles and Marty and the other characters it touches to the mood and shape of the book.

The woodland is portrayed as cruel, and winter, the season of dying, encloses the story. Man's relationship to nature is mythically embodied in John South's fears of the tree that haunts him like an evil spirit. When Giles shrouds the upper branches

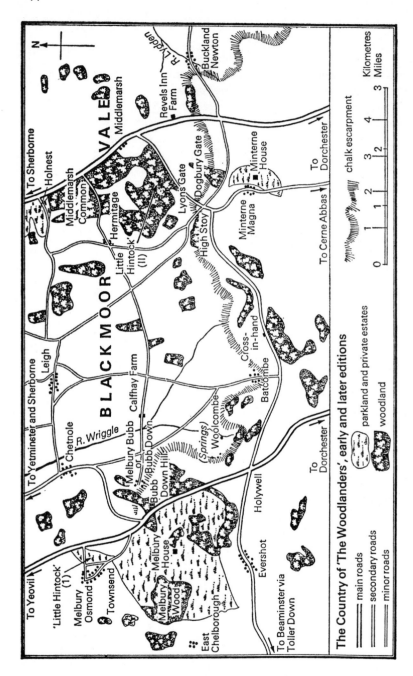

Map, *The Woodlanders* (Macmillan Publishers, Ltd)

John dies and puts into process the parallel events (the pulling down of his own cottage and his exposure to the full cruelty of the storm when propriety in the form of Grace Melbury evicts him a second time) that bring about his own death. Viewed by Grace at the point when he is shrouding the branches of John South's tree, he seems driven by a malevolent force away from her and all hope for their future. She has just rejected him as a husband:

> *He made no reply, but sat back upon a bough, placed his elbow in a fork, and rested his head upon his hand. Thus he remained till the fog and the night had completely inclosed him from her view.*

As Grace moves on with a sigh, Hardy speculates as to what she might have said to him if he had come down the tree:

> *But he continued motionless and silent in that gloomy Niflheim or fogland which involved him, and she proceeded on her way.*[23]

Hardy possessed the Golden Treasury edition of Matthew Arnold's poetry (1878) which contains the poem 'Balder Dead'. In Norse mythology Balder, the sun god and son of Odin and Frigga, is just and beautiful. Legends tell how he was protected from death by stone or wood by a spell, but eventually was killed by a sprig of mistletoe gathered from the eastern slopes of Niflheim (the edge of Hel, the underworld) by the evil Loki who then placed it in the hand of the blind Hodhr. Not knowing what he was throwing, Hodhr gave Balder his death blow. In the first section of Arnold's poem Balder's spirit returns to his wife, Nanna, and assures her that she will die soon and thus escape the agony of being burnt on his funeral pyre. He then fades away:

> *And as the woodman sees a little smoke*
> *Hang in the air, afield and disappear,*
> *So Balder faded in the night away.*[24]

Chapter three describes Marty South going out into the darkness to deliver the spar gads she has split:

> *The night in all its fullness met her flatly on the threshold, like the brink in an absolute void, or the ante-mundane Ginnung-Gap believed in by her Teutonic forefathers.*[25]

The Ginnung-Gap, in Norse mythology, is the void before the

creation of the world, one of many suggestions of the atmosphere of death that pervades Little Hintock at the beginning of the book. The rape of Marty's hair is likened to the action of Loke the Malicious who cut off the hair of Thor's wife.[26] When Grace and her father walk in the woods in chapter seven, life is absent and Hardy uses another image from Norse mythology:

> *They dived amid beeches under which nothing grew, the younger boughs still retaining their hectic leaves, that rustled in the breeze with a sound almost metallic, like the sheet-iron foliage of the fabled Jarnvid wood.*[27]

Giles, '*the fruit-God*' like Balder the good and just, must be annihilated by the destructive principle which in *The Woodlanders* and the Norse nature myth alike works the death of the year.

The two villains of the piece are Mrs Charmond and Dr Fitzpiers, the one responsible for the loss of Marty's hair and Giles's house, the other for the advice that costs John South the loss of his life and Giles the loss of his house (since the lifehold on Giles's cottage terminates with South's life). Fitzpiers is reputed to be in league with the devil and there are many suggestions of the Faust legend in which the ambitious doctor sold his soul to the devil in exchange for knowledge and power while he lived. '*They say he's in league with the devil*',[28] says a traveller on Mrs Dollery's van, and Hardy repeats the rumour in the opening of chapter two. Tangs, Melbury's top sawyer, has the same fear:

> '*I won't praise the doctor's wisdom till I hear what bargain he's made*',[29]

and Cawtree tells us how a parson's wife became hysterical when she opened a bundle of Fitzpiers's books that had been erroneously delivered to her husband. In refuting the primitive notions of his workmen, Melbury gives the reader the hint that Fitzpiers is a dilettante, ranging widely in his studies, playing with them as a cure for boredom:

> '*he's only a gentleman fond of science and philosophy, and poetry, and, in fact, every kind of knowledge; and being lonely here he passes his time in making such matters his hobby.*'[30]

Philosophically, Hardy makes him a student of German transcendental philosophy. He tells Grammer Oliver: '*Let me tell you that Everything is Nothing. There's only Me and Not me'*, yawning all the time. This failure to distinguish the outside world as having some sort of objective reality separate from the perception of Dr Fitzpiers becomes equally apparent when he quotes Spinoza at Giles Winterborne as they drive past Grace Melbury's house:

> *'Human love is a subjective thing—the essence itself of man, as that great thinker Spinoza says—* ipsa hominis essentia *—it is joy accompanied by an idea which we project against any suitable object in the line of our vision, just as the rainbow iris is projected against an oak, ash or elm tree indifferently.'*[31]

Hardy dramatizes this aspect of Dr Fitzpiers's nature in the account of Grace's visit to his house. Between sleep and wakefulness, as he lies on the sofa, he has opened his eyes once and perceived a reflection of Grace in the looking-glass. When she retreats, embarrassed, and returns a second time, he is confused between the idea of Grace that appeared to be in his mind when he woke and the real Grace who has just appeared. Flirtatiously likening her to the embodiment of the Platonic ideal form, he tells her:

> *'The design is for once carried out. Nature has at last recovered her lost union with the Idea! My thoughts ran in that direction because I had been reading the work of a transcendental philosopher last night; and I dare say it was the dose of Idealism that I received from it that made me scarcely able to distinguish between reality and fancy.*[32]

This confusion between reality and fancy is what makes him so destructive a man in the story. It is seen in his treatment of Grammer Oliver's head or, under the microscope at the end of this chapter, John South's brain, as nothing other than objects of his study; in his view of Suke Damson as an object of his lust; of Grace Melbury as an object for his romance and, since a yearning for the distant and new experience is never sated in such people, his use of Mrs Charmond as mistress. Hardy returns to the theme of idealism in his last published novel, *The Well-Beloved* (1897).

Fitzpiers is the human cause for Grace's misery, though not the only one: she is also victim of her father's ambition, her own adherence to social convention, and victim too of the divorce laws. Alone in Winterborne's hut, like Giles up the tree earlier, she is completely depersonalized:

> *She seemed almost to be apart from herself—a vacuous duplicate only. The recent self of physical animation and clear intentions was not there.*
>
> *Sometimes a bough from an adjoining tree was swayed so low as to smite the roof in the manner of a gigantic hand smiting the mouth of an adversary, to be followed by a trickle of rain, as blood from the wound.*[33]

Now the tragic power that deprives Grace of her feelings and which is killing Giles seems to be nature itself.

Mrs Charmond is also associated with the malignant natural force. Her house stands in a hole, is *'vegetable nature's own home'* and uncontrollably damp.

> *The ashlar of the walls, where not overgrown with ivy and other creepers, was coated with lichen of every shade, intensifying its luxuriance with its nearness to the ground till, below the plinth, it merged in moss.*[34]

On the walls inside are man's equivalent of nature's predatory growths, the man-traps and such articles collected by Mrs Charmond's husband. Her wry comment to Grace carries the malignance into the sexual field:

> *'Man-traps are of rather ominous significance where a person of our sex lives, are they not?'*

Just as the false locks Mrs Charmond took from Marty are to be the cause of the quarrel in which she loses her life, so too will a man-trap be the means whereby Grace and Fitzpiers are brought together at the end of the book.

For love does triumph in this novel, not so much in the awkward departure of Grace and her husband to a new life away from Little Hintock as in the reassertion of the regenerative force in Marty's eulogy over Giles's grave. We know that the malignant force which has appeared severally in the guises of mythology, winter in the woods, society, and the attitudes of individual characters, is not all that there is. Marty will continue to work Giles's cider press, the larches she plants will grow strong and her love for the individual man will remain constant in her memory.

THE MAYOR OF CASTERBRIDGE (1886)

Dr Gittings makes some interesting observations on the topicality of *The Mayor of Casterbridge*.[35] The Eddison Steam Plough Works, set up in Dorchester by a northerner in the 1870s, was well established in 1884 when Hardy started writing *The Mayor of Casterbridge*. Francis Eddison had saved the works from bankruptcy by adapting it from making steam ploughs to road-making machinery. It was manned largely by labour from the North and the Midlands. Hardy himself had complained about the noise of the factory hooter at 5.45 a.m. The elements of mechanization of agriculture, bankruptcy, northern skill and local resentment all find their way into Hardy's novel, set in the Dorchester he knew around 1850.

Excavation for the foundations of Max Gate revealed it to be a Roman burial ground. While it was being built, the Hardys rented a tiny cottage in Shirehall. In these cramped quarters, overlooking Gaol Lane, he wrote *The Mayor of Casterbridge*.

A television adaptation of the book, shown first on BBC in spring 1978, showed Farfrae and Elizabeth-Jane beside the laid-out corpse of Henchard and, ignoring the request in the will, ended with a close-up of an invented tombstone. This seemed very different from Hardy's ending, because the process of the story of Michael Henchard's life is a process towards self-destruction and annihilation. In the book, Abel Whittle is outside the house when he describes Henchard's death, and he fetches out the will which ends with the request, '*that no man remember me*'.

> *What Henchard had written in the anguish of his dying was respected as far as practicable by Elizabeth-Jane, though less from a sense of the sacredness of last words, as such, than from her independent knowledge that the man who wrote them meant what he said. She knew the directions to be a piece of the same stuff that his whole life was made of. . .*[36]

The physical absence of Henchard's body from this scene and the immediate distancing of the events by the change into retrospective reportage enact his last wishes.

Shakespeare's Othello or Emily Bronte's Heathcliff are the closest one comes in literature to the self-destructive, violent passion of Henchard, and one is not surprised to learn that Hardy had recently re-read *Othello*, but in *The Mayor of*

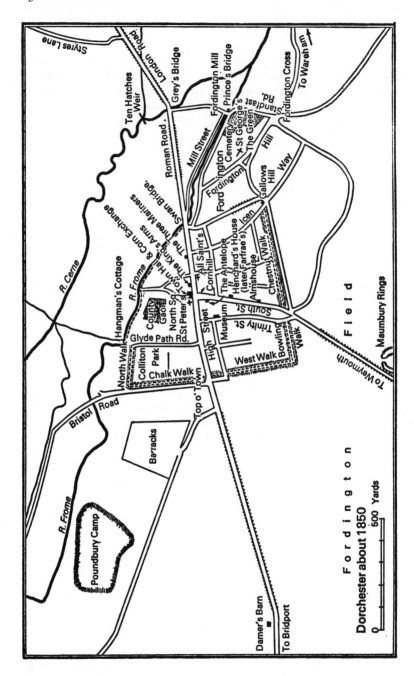

Map, *The Mayor of Casterbridge* (Macmillan Publishers, Ltd)

Casterbridge there is no Cathy and no Desdemona. Henchard's tragedy must be enacted alone.

A tragic hero must be sufficiently sympathetic for the reader or audience to care about what happens to him. How, in *The Mayor of Casterbridge*, does Hardy create and retain the reader's sympathy for a man of such violent temperament and behaviour (selling his wife, his rough treatment of Whittle, his interruption of the visit of the Royal personage, his assault on Farfrae in the granary), or with such lack of self-control (of which his drinking and temper are symptomatic), and whose gross malevolence is seen in his reading of Lucetta's love-letters to Farfrae and in his deception of Newson and Elizabeth-Jane?

None of these labels sufficiently expresses the full picture of Henchard we are given in the book. Our first view of him uses visual detail to express personal qualities: his walk is purposeful ('*the walk of the skilled countryman*') and the turn and plant of each foot express '*a dogged and cynical indifference personal to himself*'. This strength (as much physical as it is moral) is emphasized by contrast with the weakness of his wife's appearance:

> ... *she had the hard, half-apathetic expression of one who deems anything possible at the hands of Time and Chance except, perhaps, fair play.*[37]

He is out of work because there is none, rather than through indolence. Though the picture of Henchard at the end of chapter one, having sold his wife, snoring and incapably drunk, shows him at his least sympathetic, at his moral nadir in the book, we have already responded to him as a strong, purposeful character. This is now re-established in chapter two.

On emerging from the tent, '*the freshness of the Sunday morning inspired and braced him as he stood*' and, having left Weydon Priors, he leans on a gate to consider what he has done. We again feel his strong physical presence as he makes his oath. He opens the gates of the altar rail, feels the sense of the strangeness for a moment, kneels, drops his head on a clamped Bible on the communion table and makes his oath aloud. He then kisses the book and leaves the church. The cottager's newly lit fire echoes his feeling that a new start is possible. At the end of chapter two it is as much our awareness of Henchard's physical presence as his genuine contrition that evokes our response to the man.

It is easy to overemphasize the moral quality of Henchard's subsequent rise to fortune—there is nothing intrinsically noble about his working his way up to being principal figure in the community though we may admire the implied energy and purposefulness. Indeed, morally, his reply to the question about the bad bread is dubious. At that point it is again the emotional and physical violence that we notice:

> Henchard's face darkened. There was temper under the thin bland surface—the temper which, artificially intensified, had banished a wife nearly a score of years before.[38]

Morally we approve his reinstatement of Susan as his wife and of Elizabeth-Jane. But it is the depth of feeling that is involved and exposed at various moments—his first interview with Elizabeth-Jane, meeting Susan in the Ring and in his spontaneous affection for Farfrae—that opens us to the man. When he tells Farfrae about his former relationship with Susan and his later relationship with the lady from Jersey, the extent to which he is a victim of violent emotions becomes as evident as does his genuine desire to do the just thing by all concerned. He describes his condition when he first met Lucetta:

> 'Well, one autumn when stopping there I fell quite ill, and in my illness I sank into one of those gloomy fits I sometimes suffer from, on account o'the loneliness of my domestic life, when the world seems to have the blackness of hell, and, like Job, I could curse the day that gave me birth.'
> 'Ah, no, I never feel like it,' said Farfrae.[39]

Henchard's vulnerability to depression and loneliness is like the openness of his affections. We come to associate the two aspects of his personality so that even at his lowest morally we respond to the strength of his feelings. We are helped to do so by the juxtaposition of reminders of his capacity for affection: he shames Abel Whittle but keeps his mother in coals; having lost all his property in bankruptcy he sells his watch to discharge a debt to a cottager in Durnover; charged with rejection by Lucetta, and jealous of Farfrae, he reads her letters to Farfrae but cannot bring himself to reveal that it was she who sent them; and in the granary he binds his arm to give the younger man a chance and then cannot bring himself to kill him.

A further reason that we do not cease responding to Henchard sympathetically during this section of the book that charts his decline from fortune, is the element of Fate involved. The corn harvests, the reaction of Lucetta to his proposal and her subsequent marriage to Farfrae, the revelation made by the furmity woman, Newson's return—they seem out of all proportion to anything Henchard deserves. Even at his lowest, when Farfrae has ceased to trust him, Lucetta is dead, he has betrayed Elizabeth-Jane in turning Newson away and he contemplates drowning himself in the River Frome, he still has the strength to withstand the temptation. Seeing what appears to be his double floating dead in Ten Hatches Weir, he experiences a moment of self-revelation and, taking his coat and hat, he returns to Elizabeth-Jane's. In his perception of the event as a miracle ('*And yet it seems that even I be in Somebody's hand*') and in Elizabeth-Jane's returning to look after him, there are echoes of Lear's awakening to find Cordelia, the daughter he has wronged, kneeling by his side.[40]

The remainder of that year represents a period of relative peace: Newson does not return, Farfrae retains a distance from Henchard who lives with Elizabeth-Jane in the shop above the church.

> *By the end of the year, Henchard's little retail seed and grain shop, not much larger than a cupboard, had developed its trade considerably, and the stepfather and daughter enjoyed much serenity in the pleasant sunny corner in which it stood.*[41]

But with the following spring, Farfrae's affection for Elizabeth-Jane becomes evident and Henchard's stability again turns:

> ... *the* solicitus timor [anxious fear] *of his love—the dependence upon Elizabeth's regard into which he had declined (or, in another sense, to which he had advanced)— denaturalized him.*[42]

He turns to jealous enquiry into her every movement and his fear that Newson might reappear returns.

When Newson does return, there is dignity in Henchard's flight from facing what he has done. He leaves Casterbridge as he came to it, in his workman's clothes, '*Naked came I out of my mother's womb and naked shall I return thither*' is a line from the Bible story in the Book of Job with which Henchard's history has a close parallel:

> *He went secretly and alone, not a soul of the many who had known him being aware of his departure.*

Sitting down on the first milestone he accepts his loneliness as the price he must pay for his evil:

> *I—Cain—go alone as I deserve—an outcast and a vagabond. But my punishment is not greater than I can bear!*[43]

The bareness of Weydon Priors exactly echoes his desolation.

Even more complete is the desolation he feels when he returns to seek Elizabeth-Jane's forgiveness at her wedding. Having succumbed to the ties of affection once, the second departure is even more painful. When he replies to her final rejection that he will trouble her no more, not to his dying day, he admits he has been wrong and then leaves. What he has done is unforgivable, but not to forgive is still cruel: an emotional paradox that leaves us with a dead bird in a cage and one of those painful journeys we find in Hardy that are so clearly journeys of the soul towards a lonely death.

Michael Henchard retains our sympathy as tragic hero because of his ability to feel and to suffer. His rejection of Whittle's help and his will are the final examples of a man who is true to his feelings. Without the dreadful honesty in Henchard's realization that he is alone and deserves no more, we should respond to him simply as a man of violent emotion. This self-knowledge lends him a moral stature.

TESS OF THE D'URBERVILLES (1891)

We are made well aware of Tess's characterization as a child of nature. She seems one with the sun that lights her skin to the reader's view on so many occasions and the imagery she is associated with is invariably that of cats and birds, warm or vulnerable. She suffers at the hands of Fate, from the animal brutality of Alec d'Urberville, from the ethereal idealism of Angel Clare and from the conventional reaction of society to the unchaste. So far, the picture I have presented is one of a natural girl who suffers at the hands of the unnatural. However, analysis of Tess's portrayal and that of nature in the book shows a more complex picture, with the causes of Tess's fate deep in her own nature and in nature itself.

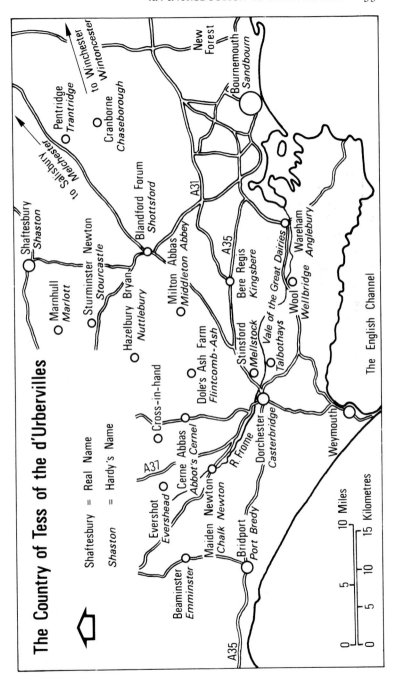

Map, *Tess of the d'Urbervilles*

Consider firstly the colour red that we are led to associate with Tess and her vitality—she wears a red ribbon in her hair at the Marlott May Day Dance; the red of her mouth is referred to twice and, when Angel kisses her arm, '*her blood was driven to her fingers end*'. But more often, the colour is associated with spilt blood and violence. The red of Tess's ribbon seen against the white of her dress is recalled in the death of the horse Prince, and, as she tries to stop the wound, the blood spurts out onto her face and skirt. Alec d'Urberville presses roses to her breast and, later, she pricks her chin on one. At the dance Tess sees the red coal of Alec's cigar and on the night of the rape she is seen as a '*white muslin figure*' sleeping on a pile of dead leaves. The rape takes place in the Vale of the White Hart where Thomas de la Lynd had killed a particularly beautiful white hart, a story that delicately allegorizes the physical rape. Alec's house, like Wintoncester Jail where she finally hangs, is also red. Having left Alec and returned to Marlott Tess works in the fields behind the reaper; the stubble pierces her arm and it bleeds.

The pheasants she finds beneath some bushes on the way to Emminster

> *... lay about, their rich plumage dabbled with blood; some were dead, some feebly twitching a wing, some staring up at the sky, some pulsating quickly, some contorted, some stretched out—all of them writhing in agony, except the fortunate ones whose tortures had ended during the night by the inability of nature to bear more.*[44]

Tess is to follow a similar path towards her eventual death. The brutality that has caused this bloodshed and suffering we have previously associated with man and nature; soon we are going to have to recognize that it is also in Tess herself when she causes Alec's blood to flow to form that scarlet blob on Mrs Brooks' ceiling with the appearance of a gigantic ace of hearts. The brutality she suffers, like the brutality of Fate itself that pierced Prince's breast, she too is capable of; similarly, the sexuality of which she is a victim is a vital part of her own nature. In the Var Valley, Angel Clare experiences '*the aesthetic, sensuous, pagan pleasure in natural life and lush womanhood*'.[45] Nor should we skimp over the four months that Tess, after her rape in The Chase, stayed at Trantridge as Alec's lover:

> *She had dreaded him, winced before him, succumbed to adroit advantages he took of her helplessness; then,*

temporarily blinded by his ardent manners, had been stirred
to confused surrender awhile ...[46]

Similarly, the sun that shines so benignantly down on the cows, crops and young lovers at Talbothays is the same sun that beats down on Tess on her long journey to Emminster, that makes scarlet the scene when she feeds the overbearing red tyrant, the threshing machine, and that finally comes up to claim his sacrifice at dawn on Midsummer Day at Stonehenge. Hardy portrays Tess in her helplessness as a small animal, depersonalized and reduced to this point at which she must submit to the consequences of her life:

> *He went to the stone and bent over her, holding one poor*
> *little hand; her breathing now was quick and small, like*
> *that of a lesser creature than a woman. All waited in the*
> *growing light, their faces and hands as if they were silvered,*
> *the remainder of their figures dark, the stones glistening*
> *green-grey, the Plain still a mass of shade. Soon the light*
> *was strong, and a ray shone upon her unconscious form,*
> *peering under her eyelids and waking her.*[47]

There are two very fine studies of *Tess of the d'Urbervilles*, the one by D. H. Lawrence[48] in which he expounds some of his central ideas about sex and beauty; the other, developing some of Lawrence's insights in a detailed critical analysis, by Tony Tanner. Having demonstrated that what happens to Tess is expressed as a process of nature, Dr Tanner comments:

> *This suggests a universe of radical opposition, working to*
> *destroy what it works to create, crushing to death what it*
> *coaxes to life. From this point of view society only appears*
> *as a fluctuating part of a larger process whereby the vertical*
> *returns to the horizontal, motion leaps into stillness and*
> *structure cedes to the unstructured.*[49]

It is in this novel that Hardy comes closest to the view of man in time expressed in the tragedies of Sophocles and Shakespeare.

JUDE THE OBSCURE (1895)

Jude the Obscure, in many ways the most disturbing of Hardy's novels to read, seems to break new ground. Here there is no seasonal structure, no regenerative force to restore love. There is no Marty South, Gabriel Oak or Giles Winterborne to speak to us of the power of faithful love. The organic agricultural communities of Mellstock, Weatherbury or the Hintocks have been superseded; the countryside of Marygreen, like Jude himself, has lost its roots and sense of personality:

> *The fresh harrow-lines seemed to stretch like the channel-lings in a piece of new corduroy, lending a meanly utilitarian air to the expanse, taking away its gradations, and depriving it of all history, beyond that of the few recent months . . .*[50]

We have come a long way from the pastoral idyll of the earlier novels.

Yet that quotation shows Hardy at his most characteristic. Here is a landscape that is at once precise historically and part of the framework of the book's symbolism, a projected landscape of the mind. Sue Bridehead claims to be motivated by rationality and quotes Mill to support her utilitarian views. Like the landscape of Marygreen she has lost touch with her deeper self. In her relationships with first the student, with Jude, and then with Phillotson, a deep fear of her own sexuality precludes her from any committed organic relationship.

So too does Christminster stand as an emblem of the tensions within Jude. He comes to perceive that this repository of wisdom and idealism is, in harsh reality, a crumbling ruin, out of touch with its original purpose and propped up financially and literally by the efforts of artisans such as him. When this fact is spelt out to him by the Master of Biblioll College he gets drunk in a low tavern in Beersheba, a run-down slum area of Christminster that corresponds to his own baser nature. The metaphorical function of the city painfully persists: the College organ playing 'Truly God is loving unto Israel' and the two clergymen discussing the significance of the eastward position at the moment that Sue and Jude find their dead children; the cheers from the remembrance games as Jude dies alone and their echo on the last page when the young men cheer the new honorary doctors: '*Ay ; young and strong-lunged! Not like our poor boy here,*' comments Widow Edlin. Religion, the great University of Christminster and Sue, in fact all the subjects of Jude's idealism, reject him.

At the centre of the book, at the point that Jude burns his classical and religious tracts (for tractarianism is his early path as utilitarianism is Sue's) and turns to Sue, there is another moment

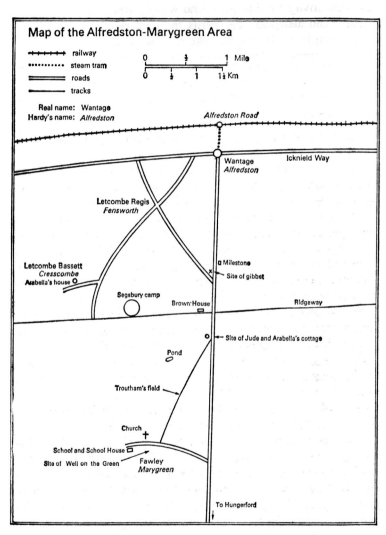

Map, *Jude the Obscure* (Macmillan Publishers, Ltd)

when the external world mirrors the private world of Jude's mind. Jude is kept awake by the cries of a rabbit caught in a snare and he must get up to put it out of its misery. Backwards in the novel it points to the sensitivity of the boy who would not tread on an earth-worm and who allowed the birds to feed on Farmer Troutham's corn. Forwards in the book, like the parallel incident of Tess and the pheasants, it prefigures Jude's own death, suffering and alone. Are not also the journeys between Marygreen, Aldbrickham, Melchester and Christminster the external equivalents of Jude's restless search for emotional and intellectual fulfilment?

The two central women can also be seen as projections of Jude's own nature. Sue Bridehead, both in her utilitarianism and her inability to explore her sexual nature, develops Hardy's earlier study of the type in Angel Clare. In her vacillating impetuosity and in her appearance she is also a development of Fancy Day and Bathsheba Everdene, but she completely lacks their sexuality. Arabella, on the other hand, mixes the full-bosomed, provocative voluptuousness of Suke Damson in *The Woodlanders* with a calculating falsity (echoed in her false braid and false pregnancy), animality (externalized by her frequent associations with pigs) and rough realism that is all her own. Professor Alvarez sees the two women in these terms:

> *Sue and Arabella are, in fact, like the black and white horses, the noble and base instincts, which drew Plato's chariot of the soul.*[51]

Sue's idealism and intellectual quest echo Jude's own, just as Arabella's animal nature calls to that part of him.

Yet the two women also have their similarities in their effect on Jude. Arabella's flirtatiousness with the cochin's egg is a sexual equivalent of Sue's later coquetry; both girls treat him with equal callousness. Both flee to him when they are in need and both bring on him his final isolation. Sue, driven by repression and guilt, returns to a loveless union with Phillotson, and Arabella, true to her sexual characterization, accompanies Vilbert to the remembrance games, leaving Jude to die alone. Sue, in flaunting convention and then succumbing to it, is a heroine who perfectly expresses the tensions of the Victorian age. Liberated from convention in both human relationships and religion she yet submits to conversion to what Hardy calls

Sacerdotalism and a sexless marriage to Phillotson. As Terry Eagleton has observed:

> *In descrying the false social embodiments of love, she denies the body itself.*[52]

In *Jude the Obscure* we find Hardy's fullest characterization of types that have pervaded his earlier novels; we find a development of themes and social criticism already explored in his earlier novels, and the most sustained example of a persistent tragic irony to be found in any of them. This last novel leaves us with a picture of a completely deracinated culture: Jude's isolation and suffering completely fill the screen. It was left to D. H. Lawrence some twenty years later to explore further the psychology of well-being and to rediscover within the family a sense of continuity in human experience. Both writers share a deep sense of compassion for the sufferings of their characters: compassion is the one quality that we find in all great writing.

[1] William Shakespeare *As You Like It* Act 2 scene 5 [2] Thomas Hardy *Under the Greenwood Tree* Autumn Chap. 5 p. 209 [3] *ibid*. Chap. 6 p. 214 [4] F. B. Pinion *A Hardy Companion* (Macmillan, 1968) pp. 187-192 [5] as 2, Autumn Chap. 2 p. 196 [6] *ibid*. Chap. 3 p. 199 [7] Thomas Hardy *Far from the Madding Crowd* Chap. 43 p. 382 [8] *ibid*. Chap. 5 p. 75 [9] *ibid*. Chap. 46 p. 403 [10] *ibid*. Chap. 3 p. 55 [11] *ibid*. Chap. 5 p. 72 [12] *ibid*. Chap. 9 p. 115 [13] *ibid*. Chap. 20 p. 187 [14] *ibid*. Chap. 46 p. 400 [15] Thomas Hardy *The Return of the Native*, Bk. 1 Chap. 2 p. 51 [16] J. Paterson 'An Attempt at Grand Tragedy' in A. E. Dyson (Ed.) *Hardy, The Tragic Novels* (Macmillan Casebook series, 1975) p. 114 [17] as 15, Bk. 1 Chap. 1 p. 45 [18] *ibid*. Bk. 4 Chap. 3 p. 342 [19] *ibid*. Bk. 1 Chap. 6 p. 111 [20] *ibid*. Bk. 3 Chap. 6 p. 284 [21] *ibid*. Bk. 3 Chap. 6 p. 286 [22] *ibid*. Bk. 3 Chap. 7 p. 291 [23] Thomas Hardy *The Woodlanders* Chap. 13 pp. 141 and 142 [24] 'Balder Dead' by Matthew Arnold lines 335-338 [25] as 23, Chap. 3 p. 45 [26] *ibid*. Chap. 3 p. 50 [27] *ibid*. Chap. 7 p. 90 [28] *ibid*. Chap. 1 p. 35 [29] *ibid*. Chap. 4 p. 62 [30] *ibid*. Chap. 4 p. 61 [31] *ibid*. Chap. 16 p. 168 [32] *ibid*. Chap. 18 p. 184 [33] *ibid*. Chap. 41 p. 401 [34] *ibid*. Chap. 8 p. 96 [35] R. Gittings *The Older Hardy* (Heinemann Educational, 1978) pp. 41-42 [36] Thomas Hardy *The Mayor of Casterbridge* Chap. 45 p. 419 [37] *ibid*. Chap. 1 p. 34 [38] *ibid*. Chap. 5 p. 73 [39] *ibid*. Chap. 12 p. 123 [40] William Shakespeare *King Lear* Act 4 scene 7; as 36, Chap. 41 [41] as 36, Chap. 42 p. 382 [42] *ibid*. Chap. 42 p. 385 [43] *ibid*. Chap. 43 p. 395 [44] Thomas Hardy *Tess of the d'Urbervilles* Chap. 41 p. 389 [45] *ibid*. Chap. 25 p. 240 [46] *ibid*. Chap. 12 p. 141 [47] *ibid*. Chap. 58 p. 543 [48] D. H. Lawrence 'A Study of Thomas Hardy' *Phoenix*, London 1936 [49] Tony Tanner 'Tess, Nature and the Voices of Hardy', reprinted in R. P. Draper (Ed.) *Hardy: The Tragic Novels* (Macmillan, 1975) p. 204 [50] Thomas Hardy *Jude the Obscure* Chap. 2 p. 48 [51] A. Alvarez 'Jude the Obscure', reprinted in A. J. Guerard (Ed.) *Hardy: A Collection of Essays* (Prentice-Hall, 1963) [52] Terry Eagleton, Preface to the New Wessex Edition of *Jude the Obscure* (Macmillan, 1975).

Bibliography

EDITIONS

The New Wessex edition of poems, short stories and novels is available both in paperback and hardback. Each volume has a critical introduction by an eminent critic (Macmillan). The cheapest edition and the best for student purposes because it contains notes, a critical introduction and is in paperback, is the Macmillan Students' Hardy. All page references in this book are to that edition. The authoritative edition of the poems is:

GIBSON, JAMES *Thomas Hardy: The Complete Poems* (Macmillan, 1976)

BACKGROUND

KAY-ROBINSON, D. *Hardy's Wessex Re-appraised* (David & Charles, 1972)
PINION, F. B. *A Hardy Companion* (Macmillan, 1968)

BIOGRAPHY

GITTINGS, R. *Young Thomas Hardy* (Penguin, 1978); *The Older Hardy* (Heinemann Educational, 1978)
GITTINGS, R. *The Second Mrs. Hardy* (Heinemann, 1979)
HARDY, F. E. *The Life of Thomas Hardy* (Macmillan, 1966)
O'SULLIVAN, T. *Thomas Hardy: An Illustrated Biography* (Macmillan, 1976)

CRITICAL STUDIES

BROWN, D. *Thomas Hardy* (Longmans, 1954)
CARPENTER, R. *Thomas Hardy* (Macmillan, 1976)
DRAPER, R. P. (Ed.) *Hardy: The Tragic Novels* (one of the Macmillan Casebook series, containing useful essays on *The Return of the Native, The Mayor of Casterbridge, Tess of the d'Urbervilles* and *Jude the Obscure*) (Macmillan, 1975)

GUERARD, A. J. (Ed.) *Hardy: A Collection of Critical Essays* (Prentice-Hall, 1963)

MILLGATE, M. H. *Thomas Hardy: His Career as a Novelist* (The Bodley Head, 1971)

STEWART, J. I. M. *Thomas Hardy* (Allen Lane, 1971); *Eight Modern Writers* (O.U.P., 1973)

WING, G. *Hardy* (Oliver & Boyd, 1963)

ON THE POETRY

BAILEY, J. O. *The Poetry of Thomas Hardy* (Chapel Hill, 1970)

HYNES, S. L. *The Pattern of Hardy's Poetry* (Chapel Hill and O.U.P., 1961)

PINION, F. B. *A Commentary on the Poems of Thomas Hardy* (Macmillan, 1976)

SOCIAL HISTORY

LEACH, R. *The Wellesbourne Tree*, A Musical Documentary Play (Blackie, 1975)

WILLIAMS, M. *Thomas Hardy and Rural England* (Macmillan, 1972)

FOLKLORE

FIROR, R. *Folkways in Thomas Hardy* (Russell & Russell, N.Y., 1968)

FILMSTRIPS

Bryanston Audiovision Ltd, in conjunction with Blackie & Son Ltd, are producing a series of filmstrips which link up with the *Authors in their Age* books. These filmstrips, which are in full colour, aim to supplement in visual terms the content of the books, and provide a further dimension to the reader's understanding of a particular author's age. Already available are filmstrips on Chaucer, Milton, and Keats and Shelley. The filmstrip on Thomas Hardy will be available on publication of this book. Further details are available from Bryanston Audiovision Ltd, 2 Portman Mews South, Portman Street, London W1H 9AU, or from Blackie & Son Ltd.

THE WORKS OF THOMAS HARDY GIVEN WITH THE DATES OF PUBLICATION

Date	Novels	Plays	Poetry	Short Stories
1871	*Desperate Remedies*			
1872	*Under the Greenwood Tree*			
1873	*A Pair of Blue Eyes*			
1874	*Far from the Madding Crowd*			
1876	*The Hand of Ethelberta*			
1878	*The Return of the Native*			
1880	*The Trumpet-Major*			
1881	*A Laodicean*			
1882	*Two on a Tower*			
1886	*The Mayor of Casterbridge*			
1887	*The Woodlanders*			
1888				*Wessex Tales*
1891	*Tess of the d'Urbervilles*			*A Group of Noble Dames*
1894				*Life's Little Ironies*
1896	*Jude the Obscure*			
1897	*The Well-Beloved* (written before *Jude the Obscure*)			
1898			*Wessex Poems and Other Verse*	
1901			*Poems of the Past and Present*	
1904		*The Dynasts* Pt. 1		

1906	*The Dynasts* Pt. 2	
1908	*The Dynasts* Pt. 3	
1909		*Time's Laughingstocks and Other Verse*
1913		*A Changed Man and Other Tales*
1914		*Satires of Circumstance (including Poems of 1912-13)*
1917		*Moments of Vision*
1922		*Late Lyrics and Earlier*
1925		*Human Shows*
1928		*Winter Words*

THE SETTINGS OF THE MAJOR WESSEX NOVELS DATED

Novel	Composition	Date of Setting	Locality
Under the Greenwood Tree	1872	circa 1840	Mellstock is Stinsford, Hardy's home parish.
The Return of the Native	1878	1847-48	The heathland stretching east of Hardy's cottage, characterized as Egdon Heath.
The Mayor of Casterbridge	1884	1850-56 main action	Dorchester (Casterbridge), the county town of Dorset.
Far from the Madding Crowd	1874	1869-73	Near Puddletown, to the north-east of Hardy's home.
The Woodlanders	1886	1876-79	Vale of Blackmore, the wooded area to the north of Dorchester, stretching to Sherborne.
Tess of the d'Urbervilles	1890	approx. 1870-80	Talbothays—a dairy farm in the Frome Valley. Flintcomb-Ash, a hill farm in the North Dorset Downs.
Jude the Obscure	1895	1890s	A village near Reading. Oxford (Christminster), Salisbury (Melchester), Reading (Aldbrickham), Shaftesbury (Shaston).

Index

Page numbers in italics refer to illustrations.